J
796.33
A

Antonacci, Robert Joseph, 1916-
Soccer for young champions / Robert J. Antonacci and Anthony J. Puglisi ; illustrated by Patti Boyd. -- New York : McGraw-Hill, [c1978.] 183p. ill.
FEB '79 6-9

SUMMARY: Discusses the history, rules, and techniques of soccer including drills, advice on keeping score, and ways of involving the physically handicapped in the sport.

ISBN 0-07-002147-3 7.95

1. Soccer.

~~99824~~ N78

77-27565
MARC AC 86

Soccer for Young Champions

Other Books in the Young Champion Series

BASEBALL FOR YOUNG CHAMPIONS, Second Edition
PHYSICAL FITNESS FOR YOUNG CHAMPIONS, Second Edition
FOOTBALL FOR YOUNG CHAMPIONS, Second Edition
TRACK AND FIELD FOR YOUNG CHAMPIONS
BASKETBALL FOR YOUNG CHAMPIONS

Soccer for Young Champions

Robert J. Antonacci
and Anthony J. Puglisi
illustrated by Patti Boyd

McGraw-Hill Book Company
NEW YORK ST. LOUIS SAN FRANCISCO AUCKLAND BOGOTÁ
DÜSSELDORF JOHANNESBURG LONDON MADRID MEXICO
MONTREAL NEW DEHLI PANAMA PARIS SÃO PAULO
SINGAPORE SYDNEY TOKYO TORONTO

Library of Congress Cataloging in Publication Data

Antonacci, Robert Joseph, date.
Soccer for young champions.

Includes glossary and index.
SUMMARY: Discusses the history, rules, and techniques of soccer including drills, advice on keeping score, and ways of involving the physically handicapped in the sport.
1. Soccer—Juvenile literature. [1. Soccer] I. Puglisi, Anthony J., joint author. II. Boyd, Patti. III. Title.
GV943.25.A6 796.33'42 77-27565
ISBN 0-07-002147-3

123456789 BPBP 78321098

Contents

Soccer for Young Champions

1
Soccer, the World Team Game

THE STARTING KICKOFF

"Ready!" shouts the referee.

He places the ball in the middle of the circle at the center of the field. Both teams are in their places and anxious to start. It's the powerful Dynamos against the speedy Cosmos . . .

Listen! There's the referee's whistle. In the stands the fans are yelling, "Go Dynamos!" "Come on Cosmos!" The game is on!

The Dynamos' kickoff player passes the ball to a teammate. The Cosmos' striker moves forward to intercept. Mike, the Dynamos' tricky dribbler, changes the direction and avoids the tackle.

Like a flash, Mike makes an outside-of-the-foot pass to a Dynamo teammate. From out of nowhere, Dave the Cosmos' quick midfielder, steps in and intercepts the pass with his foot. After a short dribble, he sends the ball zooming to a teammate near the opponent's goal.

The crowd is on its feet! Women and men, boys and girls, are jumping up and down. Will the Cosmos score? Will the goalkeeper block the ball?

With a mighty jump, Terry of the Cosmos shows

perfect timing. As he leaps through the air, whack! He hits the ball with his head and sends it toward the goal.

The swift and sure-handed Dynamos' goalkeeper quickly dives for the ball and catches it. Then he falls and rolls on the ground. A possible score is stopped. The crowd settles down once again.

This is soccer as it is played the world over. But how different it is from the game that was played long ago.

SOCCER IN OTHER LANDS

Kicking the Skull. Soldiers in ancient China supposedly played a game by kicking around either a leather ball or an animal skull. Historians believe that a similar kicking game was also played by young men in ancient Greece and Rome. The soldiers of Julius Caesar would introduce this game to the people of the British Isles.

Hundreds of years later, in England, young men working in the fields dug up some animal skulls. They kicked these skulls along the ground and as time passed, this became a game. A group of young players would try to kick a skull past another group. The game came to be called "kicking the skull." But the skulls were hard, and they hurt the players' feet, so the young people stuffed animal bladders and kicked them instead. The players would kick a bladder from one town to the next.

Mob Football. Kicking the skull became so popular in early England that as many as 500 players from different villages often took part in one competition. There were many injuries and even some deaths in this dangerous game, which was known in England as "mob football."

Games Come to a Halt. Around the year 1170, King Henry II called a halt to mob football because his soldiers were spending too much time on the sport instead of learning how to fight. More than a century later, in 1365, King Edward III decided to end all football games. It was James I, in 1603, who returned the game to the people. Associations throughout the British Isles then began to form their own teams and rules.

Soccer Gets a Name. By 1801 "association football" was being played widely. To make the game safer, each team marked a definite goal line and decided upon a definite number of players. The name "soccer" came about as people altered association to "soc," "socker," and finally to "soccer."

A Soccer Mistake. As you will learn later, soccer players must never run with the ball in their hands, except in one or two special cases. Back in the early days of the game, as today, the ball could be kicked, and players could use their heads, knees, or chests—but not their hands—to stop the ball or move it along.

It was during a soccer game played at the Rugby School in England in 1823 that one excited player made a mistake. The player *picked up* the ball and ran with it toward the goal for a score. It was an exciting moment for all! In time, other schools allowed their players to run with the ball in their hands. The game was named "rugby's football," which became "rugby football," and in time "rugby."

MORE SOCCER HISTORY

Early Goal Posts. There were no goal posts in the earliest soccer matches. A team usually scored a victory when it got the ball into its opponent's village or across a designated line. Around the year 1800, opposing teams blocked out a field and each team drove two sticks about two to three feet apart at each end to serve as goals.

TEAM CAPTAINS
AND REFEREE 1912

EARLY SOCCER GAME 1868

There were no crossbars connecting the upright posts or sticks. Some teams used tape or twine in place of more sturdy material for the crossbars. Wooden crossbars first began to be used in 1875 in London.

Goalkeepers Use Their Hands. At first goalkeepers were not allowed to put their hands on the ball. Around 1870, many years after the famous game at Rugby happened and the idea of running with the ball had been introduced, soccer rules began to permit the goalkeepers to use their hands to stop a ball from going into the scoring area. Many more years later goalkeepers were also told that they must wear a different color uniform from the rest of their teammates.

Early Uniforms. Players wore colorful uniforms in the early matches. English players in 1872 wore white jerseys with the badge of England on the left breast, dark blue caps, white knickers that fastened over their stockings below the knees, and heavy ankle-high shoes. Scots played in dark blue jerseys with the badge of a Scottish lion, white knickers, heavy shoes, white stockings, and red cowls (hoods) as headgear.

Use of Shinguards and Goal Nets. Many early players complained of getting kicked in the shins by opposing players. In about 1882 a player on England's Nottingham Forest team invented *shinguards* and wore them for the first time for protection in a game against Scotland.

To speed up the game, the goal net was invented by J. A. Brodie of Liverpool, England. It was first used in a match at Nottingham in January of 1891. These nets were secured to the back portion of the goal posts and crossbar, as they are today. Much time was saved by not having to chase the ball when it went into the goal.

SOCCER IN AMERICA

Colonial Period. Soccer was brought to America by the English. During the Colonial days in America, youngsters played a kicking game that was very much like soccer-football in England. They used a round ball; there were no fixed rules or any set number of players; team play and strategy was seldom observed in a game. John Adams, the second President of the United States, played in unorganized games of football when he was a young boy. The game he played was really soccer with

FIRST MATCH OF BRITISH LADIES FOOTBALL CLUB 1895

the ball made out of a bladder filled with air or a leather bag stuffed with rags or sawdust.

First Soccer Games. During the early years of the nineteenth century there were no organized teams. Students formed "pickup" teams and began to challenge one another at the universities of Princeton, Harvard, Yale, Amherst, Brown, and Rutgers.

Princeton students formed several teams in 1820 and

scheduled games among themselves. The playing was rough. Harvard students began playing each other in 1827 in a game called "Bloody Monday." This name was chosen because the game was played on the first Monday on every new school year, and many students would come off the field with sore shins, black eyes, missing teeth, and bloody noses. It was much later before students played on organized teams.

The first organized *high school teams* developed around 1860 in Boston. Now that the round ball was beginning to be accepted, the players started to show better passing and dribbling skills. The Civil War, however, put a stop to much of the competition in schools and colleges.

In 1869 a Princeton team played against Rutgers. This was the first football game played by two American colleges in the United States. It was played under soccer rules and was not like football today.

In 1873 the first soccer-football game played in the United States by an American team against a team from another country took place between players from Yale University and players from the Eton School in England. For the first time eleven players were used on a team. Eleven players are used today!

Playing Positions Are Named. In 1869 Princeton University had a rule allowing 25 players on a team. Around this time most teams in England and the United States began to limit the number of players to eleven on a team. The team was made up of nine forwards and two defenders. This was the beginning of the use of special team plays and formations.

Scoring System. During Colonial times the team that put the ball across a line a few miles away, or into the next village, won the game. But there was no set rule on how to score or declare a winner. In the early college games, the team scoring six goals won the match. Later, the rules were changed so a game would last a specified length of time and each goal scored would give one point. The team with the most points won.

Soccer Ball Comes of Age. You have already learned that centuries ago the earliest soccer balls were animal skulls or bladders. Next, rubber was used to make a stronger bladder, but it was difficult to keep the ball round during the game and there was no set size.

In a game between Princeton and Rutgers in 1861, it was difficult, as usual, to keep the ball completely round throughout the match. Players had to take turns blowing air into the ball, and, as a result, the game had to be stopped several times to fill the bladder and make it round again.

In 1867 H. A. Alden of Matteawan, New York, invented the first soccer ball covering. The bladder was still made of rubber, but now it was covered with canvas to make a stronger ball. Today only the finest quality leather and rubber material is used to control the size and weight of the ball.

SOCCER ASSOCIATIONS AND LEAGUES

In 1848 representatives from schools in England met at Trinity College to outline the *first set of amateur soccer rules.*

Interest in the game encouraged individual players to organize their own teams and form clubs so they could play for money. The clubs soon began to buy players away from each other. In 1885 twelve of these clubs met and formed the Professional Football League of England.

1891

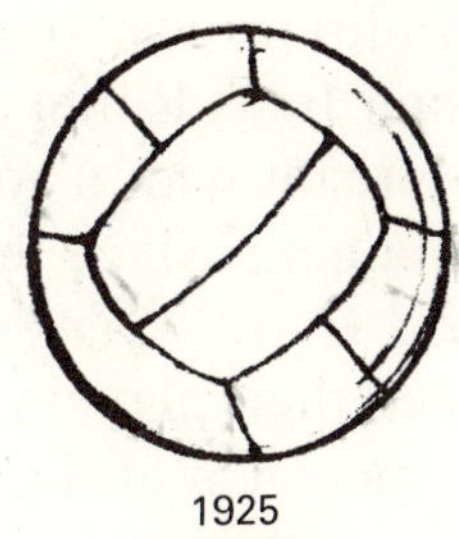

1925
MODERN

1962
MODERN

SOCCER BALLS

The Federation International Football Association. In the late nineteenth century, each nation had its own associations and rules. Rivalries between countries became rowdy and even fierce. In one big game between Scotland and England at Ibrox Park, Glasgow in 1903, an overcrowded section of the stands collapsed—twenty-five fans were killed and 300 others injured. This sad event inspired the different countries to organize the *Federation International Football Association*, or the F.I.F.A., in 1904. Today the organization continues to see that all nations follow the same soccer rules.

The Olympic Games. Amateur soccer players from every country wanted a chance to compete in the Olympic Games, which are held every four years. In 1900 soccer teams from the different countries got their wish and took part in the Olympics for the first time.

The World Cup. People from every corner of the world believe that the World Cup soccer competition is the biggest sports attraction of all. Each country's very best amateur and professional players are selected to play on its World Cup team. This team represents the country in the competition, which is held every four years.

The World Cup tradition was started in Montevideo, Uruguay in 1930, when Jules Rimet of France presented the winning Uruguay team with a gold cup at the end of an international tournament. Since that day the event has had the name "World Cup." Many of the participating countries have honored their players, team, and the game of soccer by issuing special World Cup postage stamps.

Immigrants and Soccer Clubs. Around 1900 immigrants from many countries began to settle in the United States, and they formed their own soccer clubs in the cities where they settled. These teams kept the interest in soccer alive and helped to spread the game to schools and colleges.

Soccer Keeps Growing. In 1913 the United States Football Association was formed to control the game of soccer in America. The name was changed in 1945 to United States Soccer Football Association. Today it is known as the *United States Soccer Federation.*

After World War I the game of soccer caught on in more schools and colleges and in 1926 the *Intercollegiate Soccer Football Association of America* was formed. This group is still going strong under the direction of the National Collegiate Athletic Association (N.C.A.A.).

The *National Association for Girls' and Womens' Sports* and the *National Federation of State High School Associations* are other sponsors of soccer matches and help train officials and teachers.

Amateur Competition. Today elementary schools, recreation centers, and thousands of neighborhood soccer clubs have teams for players young and old. High school teams belong to leagues or conferences and play for conference and state championships. Factory and business organizations often sponsor teams and form leagues.

"All-American." The dream of many college players is to be chosen as a player on an "All-American" team. At the end of every soccer season an All-American College team is selected. High school players make an "All-Conference" or "All-State" team.

Indoor Soccer. Soccer can also be played indoors. Some professional teams have already done this because it gives many fans an opportunity to see games without worrying about the weather. The indoor rules are different, however. Six to seven players make up a team, and the playing "field" and scoring areas are smaller.

Schools and colleges often play a form of soccer indoors when the weather is bad or there is a lack of space outdoors. However, it is very important that a safe indoor area is selected for play. Windows, lights, and spectators must be protected.

Soccer on the Move. On June 19, 1977, the professional North American Soccer League game between the New York Cosmos and the Tampa Bay Florida Rowdies drew a crowd of 62,344 fans, a record in the United States. On August 14, 1977, the Cosmos played the Fort Lauderdale Florida Strikers before a crowd of 77,691 fans for a North American record. Both games were held at the Giants Stadium in East Rutherford, New Jersey.

Other Soccer-type Games. There are small schools, colleges, and clubs that do not have enough players for a regular soccer team. Some players cannot afford to buy uniforms. Others cannot find a regulation-size field. To make it possible for such groups to enjoy the game, other forms of soccer are available. These offshoots use fewer players, a smaller playing field, and shorter playing time, but the game itself is just the same as regular soccer.

Today doctors, teachers, coaches, parents, and city officials are making it possible for young boys and girls, men and women, to take an active part in soccer. The game skills are being taught to students in schools, colleges, and on playgrounds. Height and weight make no difference in playing a good soccer game or having fun. Many of the most outstanding soccer players in the world are short. One of the most popular players of all time is Pelé, a former Cosmos team player, who is five feet, six inches tall.

2
Know Your Soccer

Go to soccer games. Watch the games on TV or listen to them on the radio. Read about soccer in newspapers, magazines, and books. As you watch, listen, and read, you will see that soccer demands both brains and physical skill.

One team is the attackers; they have possession of the ball. The opposing team is the defenders; they try to defend their goal. The attackers move the ball into the defender's territory. They make accurate foot passes and dribble their way through the defenders. The attackers want to score a goal! But the defending team fights back. They try to capture the ball. This is soccer!

To enjoy a game it is necessary to understand it. After you get to know soccer, no doubt you will qualify as a *specialist* and will be able to tell others how to play.

BEFORE THE GAME

Is your favorite team going to play? Who are the players? What are their playing records? What is the record of their team?

Read the newspapers and learn the numbers of the

players, their positions, and their ages, heights, and weights. Sports writers in newspapers and magazines often give such information about soccer players and teams.

THE PLAYING FIELD

The size of the playing field changes with the age of the players and the league they represent. On each end of the field stand the goal posts.

Professional. These fields range from 100 yards to 130 yards long and from 50 to 100 yards wide.

College. These fields are from 110 to 120 yards long and from 65 to 75 yards wide.

High School—Boys. Boys' fields are from 100 to 120 yards long and 65 to 75 yards wide. Approved also for girls by the National Federation of State High School Athletic Associations (NFSHSA).

High School—Girls. Girls' fields range from 80 to 100 yards long and from 40 to 60 yards wide. Approved by the National Association for Girls and Women in Sports (NAGWS).

Junior High School—Boys. The boys' fields are from 100 to 120 yards long and 55 to 75 yards wide. (Approved also for girls by the NFSHSA.)

Junior High School—Girls. The girls' fields are from 80 to 100 yards long and from 40 to 60 yards wide. (Approved by the NAGWS.)

Elementary School—Girls and Boys. Girls' and boys' fields are from 60 to 100 yards long and from 40 to 50 yards wide.

THE PLAYERS

There are eleven players on a soccer team. Each player has a definite position. Leagues and teams do not always assign the same names to each of the player positions. The positions are:

Attackers—also called strikers, forwards, and wings.
Defenders—also called fullbacks, backs, and halfbacks.
Midfielders—also called left, right, and center halfbacks, or linkmen.
Goalkeeper—also called goalie or keeper.

LENGTH OF GAME

Most college and professional soccer games last ninety minutes of actual playing time. The game is divided into two periods called "halves." Each half lasts forty-five minutes. After the first half the teams get ten minutes rest off the field. The National Federation of State High School Associations (NFSHSA) game rules for boys and girls have forty-minute halves. With permission of each team, they may divide the game into four equal quarters of twenty minutes each. Game periods for *junior high school boys and girls* may be shortened by each state high school association or by permission of both team coaches before a game. The National Association for Girls and Women in Sport (NAGWS) game rules for *junior and senior high school girls* are divided into ten-minute quarters with two-minute rest periods after the first and third quarters, and ten minutes after the second quarter. The *elementary school game for girls and boys* is divided into six-minute quarters. Players have a one-minute rest after the first and third quarters and ten minutes after the second quarter.

WARM-UP PRACTICE

Before a game, the players have warm-up practice. Every field has a different surface, so this is the time to learn how fast the ball moves when you pass it to a teammate. The whole squad, even the substitutes, turn out on the field before the game. The attackers, or strikers, dribble and make accurate shots with their feet and heads. The defenders, or backs, practice trapping, passing, and taking defensive stances against a tricky dribbler from their team. The midfielders drill on both attacking and defensive skills. The goalkeepers practice blocking and catching the ball in front of the goal.

GETTING READY FOR THE KICKOFF

The referee calls the team captains to the center of the field to decide which team will kick off. The referee tosses a coin into the air. If the winner of the toss chooses to kick off, then the loser has the choice of which goal to defend during the first half of the game.

THE KICKOFF

Both teams line up on the field. Each player is on his or her half of the field. The referee places the ball at the very center of the field. The team that selected to play the ball will make the kickoff. Players on the other team must be at least ten yards from the ball until the kickoff is made. The whistle is blown to signal the start of the game. The kicker eyes the ball, and with a quick, accurate foot pass sends it to a teammate. Play is on!

GOAL TO GO

The fans roar. They know that the team with the ball is on the move. The players are attacking forward with quick foot and head passes. They control the ball and move with snappy foot dribbling. This is a team on *offense* trying to work its way across the field to their opponent's goal for a score.

BLOCK IT! GET THAT BALL!

The fans yell for their favorite players to stop the offensive team's attack. Players without the ball run to good positions and use their skills to block or intercept the ball from their opponents. They show good *defense* in preventing their opponents from scoring.

A team may have possession of the ball one second and lose it the very next second. Players attacking and moving toward the goal for a score may suddenly find themselves on defense. Players on defense may quickly find themselves on offense, driving toward their opponent's goal. This is the kind of offensive and defensive action the fans want to see—players always on the alert.

POINTS IN SCORING

In soccer there are several ways in which a team may score a goal.

1. A goal from the *open field.*
2. A goal from a *direct free kick.*
3. A goal from a *penalty free kick.*
4. A goal from a *corner kick.*
5. A goal from a *drop ball.*

All goals count as one point. A goal is scored when the *entire ball* goes over the line between the two upright posts and under the crossbar into the net.

RESTARTING PLAY AFTER A SCORE

After each score the game is restarted with a kickoff at the center of the field, just as at the beginning of the game. The team that was scored upon takes the kickoff.

SCORING FROM AN OPEN FIELD

It is a thrill to see a player send the ball into the goal! In every game, scoring a goal from any part of the field is an exciting play. A goal from the open field can be made in several ways.

1. By kicking the ball into the goal.
2. By sending the ball into the goal with the use of the head.
3. By striking or sending the ball into the goal with other parts of the body, such as the knee, thigh, or chest, but without using the hands or arms.

GOALS FROM A FREE KICK

If a team breaks the rules, it must pay a penalty. An official may decide that a player committed a serious foul for such violations as pushing, holding, or tripping. The official will blow a whistle after seeing the foul and give the opposing team a *free kick* from the spot of the foul. If the foul took place outside the *penalty area*, a *direct free kick* is taken. A direct free kick means that a player can try to score a goal *directly* with the kick. Defending players form a "wall" ten yards away between the kicker and the goal, which makes scoring from this play difficult.

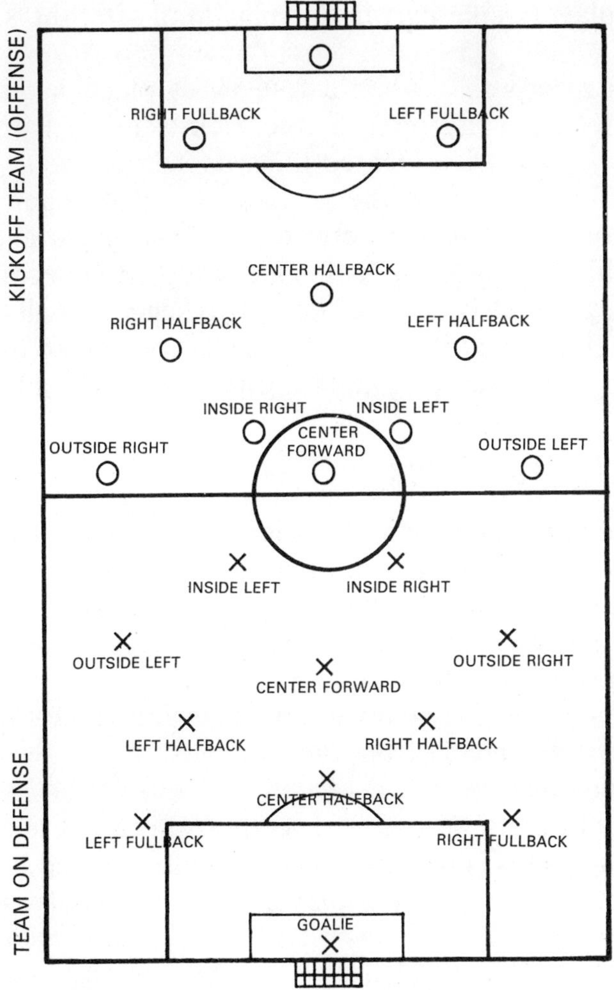

SAMPLE POSITION OF PLAYERS ON BOYS' KICKOFF

If the foul happens in the penalty area, a *penalty free kick* is taken. The penalty area is located at each end of the field. It covers an area of 44 yards along the middle of each goal line and continues 18 yards into the playing field to form a rectangle. Trying to score from a penalty free kick is very difficult. It becomes a battle of wits between the opposing goalkeeper and the kicker. No other players take part in this play until after the kick is made.

This means that when a foul takes place *within* the defender's penalty area, a free kick is taken from the penalty spot marker located 12 yards from the goal. Once the ball is placed on the ground, the goalkeeper must stand on the goal line between the goal posts and not move his feet until the ball is kicked. It soon becomes a guessing game! Will the kicker try to send the ball to the right? Or to the left? Will the goalkeeper make a swift dive to stop a score? The fans enjoy this battle of wits.

INDIRECT FREE KICK

An *indirect free kick* is awarded after a player breaks certain rules of the game. Some of these fouls are:

1. Playing too dangerously.
2. Questioning the decision of the referee.
3. Showing unsportsmanlike conduct.
4. Going onto the field without reporting to the official.
5. Trying to coach from the sidelines.
6. Being offside.

A goal cannot be scored directly from an indirect free kick play. This is because once the ball is kicked it must be touched by another player before a goal can be scored.

CORNER KICK

When the ball is last touched by a defensive player who accidently sends it traveling over the end line, but not into the goal, a *corner kick* is awarded to the offensive team. This means that the ball is placed on the ground within the quarter-circle marker located at the nearest corner flag post. Opposing players must stand at least ten yards away from the ball until it is kicked. While taking a corner kick, the kicker may try to score directly, which is very difficult, or s/he can pass to a teammate.

A corner kick in a *girls' game* is made from a marker on the goal line located five yards from the corner flag. The defending team halfbacks, fullbacks, and goalkeeper must stand on or behind the goal line until the kick is made. The attacking forwards may take any position on the field as long as they are five yards or more from the ball.

DROP BALL

A referee stops the game for a short time when s/he cannot decide which player last touched the ball before it went out of bounds. The game may also be halted for reasons that are not covered by the rules of the game. When this happens, the game is restarted by calling for a *drop ball.* If the game is stopped in the penalty area, the ball is moved to the nearest spot outside the penalty area. The referee asks for one player from each team to face a member of the other team. The players are alert, waiting for the referee to *drop the ball* between them. The kick for the ball is made as soon as it touches the ground. A goal may be scored directly from a drop ball kick, but it is difficult to do so.

OFFSIDE

When you are at your opponent's end of the field you must have two opponents between yourself and the goal line at the time the ball is played to you. You are *offside* if you receive the ball without this number of players between you and the goal line. The rule prevents the attacking (offensive) players from "hanging around" the scoring area, hoping to get a "cheap" goal. The penalty for breaking this rule is an indirect kick by one of the opposing team's players.

THROW-IN

A throw-in is called for when a player makes the entire ball go out of bounds over the sideline (touch line). A player from the opposing team is given the ball to put it back into play with a throw-in at the spot where the ball crossed the sideline. The player taking the throw-in must keep both feet on the ground, either behind or on the line, until after the ball is released. This player faces the field and holds the ball with both hands behind his or her head to make an accurate and sharp throw to a teammate. Both hands must be used to throw the ball into the playing area. The ball is brought forward over the head.

If the throw is not made properly, you do not get another chance. The referee will give the other team an opportunity to select a player to throw the ball into play.

To get more power into the throw-in, some players make a short run before throwing. However, the real force of the throw comes from the vigorous action of the wrists, elbows, arms, shoulders, and a swift swing forward of the upper body from the waist.

A goal cannot be scored directly from a throw-in.

TACKLING AND BLOCKING

A *tackle* in soccer means that you *use your feet* to take the ball away from an opponent.

A block means that you can use any part of the body to stop a ball in the air except outstretched hands and arms. When a girl uses her chest to block, she should hold her arms against her chest. Soccer skills are much different from those used in American football.

THROW-IN

TRAPPING

A *trap* means that you bring the ball under your control. For a moving ball on the ground, you may use any part of the foot. For a ball in the air, you may use any part of your body except the hands and arms.

HEADING

Heading is when a field player strikes the ball with his or her forehead. This is probably the only game in which you do not catch a ball, swing at a ball with your hands, or dodge a ball when it is coming straight for your head. In soccer you use part of your head as a "weapon." One of the most exciting plays to witness in soccer is the sight of a skilled player throwing his or her body through the air to strike the ball with the head.

DRIBBLING

Dribbling is a way of moving the ball along the ground past your opponents with your feet while keeping the ball close to you and under control. This is one of soccer's most exciting skills, as you will learn later.

SHOULDER CHARGING

A player in control of the ball can be *charged with the shoulder* by a defending player, but not violently. A legal charge is made when both players are running shoulder to shoulder and are in an upright position. They must have one foot on the ground during the actual charge which consists of a "nudge" with the near shoulder as both players try for possession of the ball.

TIE GAMES AND EXTRA PERIODS

When a game ends in a tie, it is up to the two opposing teams or their association to decide how to handle the situation. If additional playing time is decided upon, two extra periods are played. Before the start of the second period the teams change sides to defend opposite goals. The game still remains a tie if one team does not make more goals than its opponent during overtime. Sometimes the team that has taken the most corner kicks is awarded the game. Other times, penalty kicks are taken to decide the game. Or one-on-one situations can be used to settle a tie game. Whichever method is used, each team should have an equal opportunity to score.

TIME-OUTS

There are no formal time-outs in soccer, but a referee may call a time-out when a player is injured or if the referee believes it is needed for some other reason. The two teams can also decide before the game to allow for a specific number of time-outs. If a referee stops a game in play, it is restarted by a drop ball.

SUBSTITUTIONS

Only in recent years have substitutions been allowed in a soccer game. Now teams can make any number of player substitutions during a game. The only requirement is that the two teams or league agree on the rule before the game begins. Substitutes stand along the sidelines until they get the referee's attention. They must be called into the game by the referee or umpire.

3
Kicking and Shooting

You will remember that soccer started as a kicking game. Although the game has changed a great deal, kicking is still very important. What are the different kicks? How are they made? When are they used?

There are many different ways of kicking the ball. These are the most popular and the most important for you.

SOCCER KICKS

1. Instep
2. Pivot instep
3. Inside of foot
4. Outside of foot
5. Volley
6. Half-volley
7. Heel
8. Toe
9. Hitch (overhead)

Does this list look like too much to learn and remember? Don't be discouraged, because you will find that once you learn a few of the basic and most popular kicks, the others will soon become much easier. Practice one kick at a time and learn it well before moving on to another.

WHAT A KICKER MUST KNOW

A successful kick can turn defeat into victory in soccer. The kick pass is used to get the ball moving from one teammate to another, always toward the opponent's goal area. The kick shot is used to put the ball into the opponent's goal for a score.

Good players always use different kicks for better accuracy in sending the ball to a chosen target, whether it is a teammate or goal. Some players will use a special kick to make the ball curve away from an opponent standing between the kicker and the receiver. There are special kicks to help control the ball and keep it low or high. A good rule to remember is that high kicks are not always the best in soccer. The crossbar holding the goal net is only eight feet high and the ball must go *under* the crossbar to score. You will discover that a ball kicked high to a teammate will often give the opponent a better chance to steal or intercept it because it is in the air longer.

To become a good kicker you must know how to:

1. Decide quickly which kick to use.
2. Keep your eyes on the ball.
3. Take the kicker's stance for the kick you decide to use.
4. Take the approach steps before the kick.
5. Balance on one foot while the other foot is about to make the kick.
6. Make the correct foot contact when meeting the ball for your chosen kick.
7. Follow through on the kick.
8. Get yourself free from an opponent after the kick pass.

Write this information in your *Soccer Notebook.*

You may kick the ball from a *stationary* position or

from a *running* position. Either foot can be used to kick. Practice the kicks with your strongest foot first, then begin to work on them with your other foot.

This is the kind of practice that will make you a better player and that helps to win games.

INSTEP KICK

The instep kick is used more than any other kind of kick. When the ball is stationary and you want it to travel straight ahead, this is what you do:

Approach for the Kick

a. Start approaching the ball with comfortable steps.
b. Take one last regular-size step with the foot not doing the kicking. Place it about six-to-ten inches directly alongside the ball.
c. Bend your kicking foot behind you, ready to make the kick. Continue to keep your eyes on the ball.

The Kick

a. Bend the knee of your kicking leg behind you.
b. Start the forward motion of the kick at the hip.
c. Your eyes and knee should be in a straight line directly over the ball when your body shifts forward. All your weight is now on the foot on the ground.
d. The toe of the kicking foot is pointed downward and slightly inward.
e. Now comes the kick! With a nice forward "whipping" knee action, your foot meets the center of the ball with the instep, or the lace portion of your shoe.
f. Your leg is straight as your foot strikes the ball.

1) APPROACHING BALL

2) THE KICK
INSTEP KICK

3) FOLLOW-THROUGH

Kick Follow-through. The *follow-through* should end with the kicking foot pointed toward your target, or where you want to place the ball. Begin to lean back slightly after the forward "whipping" motion of the kick. This may force your other foot, which is on the ground, to raise up on the toe and make you take a short hop forward. A good follow-through will mean extra power for the kick.

PIVOT INSTEP KICK

This kick is good for propelling the ball toward the side of the field opposite your kicking foot.

1. Start toward the ball and let the foot you won't use for kicking land about eight-to-twelve inches along-

1) READY FOR PIVOT 2) READY FOR KICK

PIVOT INSTEP KICK

side and slightly behind the ball. This foot will be your *pivot foot.*

2. The kicking foot is behind you while you lean back a little toward the side of the field where the ball is to be kicked.
3. Start turning your body in the direction of the kick by *pivoting*, or turning, on the front portion of the foot on the ground.
4. At the same time, start to move your kicking leg forward from the hip. The leg begins swinging around in a circular sweeping motion.
5. As the instep of your foot meets the ball, the toes of that foot should be on the opposite side of the ball.
6. The follow-through should have your kicking foot and body facing in the direction you are aiming the ball.
7. The foot on the ground continues to *pivot* while you turn your body in the same direction and lean back slightly at the finish.

Young players enjoy practicing this kick. By striking the ball below its center, they can put a backspin on the kick. This will cause the ball to rise rapidly. It is also called a *chip shot.*

INSIDE-OF-THE-FOOT KICK

This kick is good for control in sending the ball in the direction you want it to go. It is the most widely used kick in passing to a teammate. However, it is not the best kick for getting long distance or power.

1. Start your approach steps toward the ball and place the foot that is not doing the kicking about six-to-ten inches alongside the ball.
2. Start leaning a bit forward and away from the kicking foot.

INSIDE-OF-FOOT KICK

3. Get the kicking leg behind you and begin to turn the foot outward and slightly upward. Keep your weight on the foot not doing the kicking.
4. Start bringing the kicking foot forward with good knee action, and strike the ball with the *inside* of the foot.
5. Continue to straighten the knee and follow through with the inside of the foot facing the target or the direction you want the ball to travel.

OUTSIDE-OF-THE-FOOT KICK

This kick is used to make short passes toward the outside of the foot making the kick.

1. As you approach the ball, place the nonkicking foot well behind the ball and eight-to-twelve inches to the side of it.

OUTSIDE-OF-FOOT KICK

2. Turn the kicking foot downward and inward, toward the nonkicking foot.
3. Straighten the kicking leg.
4. Strike the ball with the outside of the foot near the little toe area.
5. Make a short follow-through, with the kicking foot moving in the direction the ball is to go.
6. Immediately step down on the kicking foot to regain balance.

The farther inward your kicking foot is turned, the straighter the ball will go forward. This kick is used in rapid dribbling.

VOLLEY KICK

A *volley* means that the ball is kicked while it is in the air. You may want to use this kick when you do not have the time to stop and control, or trap, the ball because an opposing player is nearby. This situation often forces you to kick the ball away in a hurry. Other players use it to get quick height or low drives.

1. Move swiftly and position yourself a little behind the spot where you feel the fly ball will land.
2. Plant the foot not used for kicking slightly behind and to the outside of where the ball is about to drop. *Keep your eyes on the ball.*
3. Lean a bit backward, with your head pushed forward about even with the knee of the leg on the ground.
4. The kicking foot is back and ready to come forward. Keep your weight on the other foot while your arms are raised outward for balance.

VOLLEY KICK

1) MEETING THE BALL 2) FOLLOW-THROUGH

5. Strike the ball behind and slightly underneath with the instep of your foot *before the ball hits the ground.*
6. Make the follow-through with good knee action as you did for the regular instep kick.

To get greater height on the ball, just lean backward and meet the ball farther underneath. If you want low drives, lean forward a little and strike the ball just *before* it hits the ground, keeping your toes and foot facing inward and downward. If you want greater accuracy and less power, use the inside of the foot to volley kick.

HALF-VOLLEY KICK

The *half-volley* means that the ball is kicked *quickly* just *after* it hits the ground. This kind of kick usually gives you low, long drives. To get more height, strike the ball farther underneath.

1. Approach the ball in the same way as you did for the volley kick.
2. Strike the ball with the instep as soon as it touches the ground, and lean a little farther over the ball than you did for the volley kick.
3. Follow through as you did for the volley kick.

As you can see, it takes timing and practice to make this kick. Practice this kick by dropping the ball from your hands, and make contact with the ball just after it hits the ground.

HEEL KICK

The *heel* kick means that the ball is kicked backward while you are facing straight ahead. The kick goes only a short distance and it is usually not very accurate.

1. Place the foot that is not doing the kicking directly alongside the ball.

HALF-VOLLEY KICK

2. The kicking foot passes a few inches over and slightly in front of the ball. The knee is in a bent position.
3. Quickly strike the ball with the *heel* in a *backward kick*. Facing straight ahead, keep your balance by making a follow-through in which you land on the kicking foot.

   Young players rarely use this kick, but it is best used to surprise an opponent.

TOE KICK

This kick is usually made when the ball is stationary. Younger players sometimes use it for taking free kicks, corner kicks, or goal kicks. Accuracy is difficult to attain with this kick.

1. Make the last step of the foot not kicking land alongside the ball.

2. Keep the sole of your kicking foot even with the ground just before you are ready to meet the ball.
3. With the kicking foot pointing straight ahead, strike the ball just below its center with the *toe* portion of the foot.
4. Make a long follow-through by straightening the knee and swinging the leg upward.

This kick is not recommended for frequent use because accuracy is very important for your team. However, on wet days, when the ball is heavy and distance is required, the toe kick may be effective.

HEEL, OVERHEAD, HITCH KICKS

Use any type kick to clear the ball out of trouble or to score a goal. Spend most of your practice time on the instep and pivot instep kicks, inside and outside of the foot kicks, and the volley and half-volley kicks. As you grow older and stronger you may wish to work on the heel, overhead, and hitch kicks. Your teacher or coach will help you decide when you are ready to use these kicks.

HELPFUL HINTS

Begin your practice sessions with the ball in a *stationary* position. Keep your eyes on the ball at all times.

When the ball is *moving away from you*, the foot not doing the kicking should land a little ahead of the ball.

On a ball *moving toward you*, the ground foot should land a little toward the back of the ball.

Know the speed at which you must move to get into the right position for the kick you want to make.

Know what kicks are best for you when going after

the ball from a side, angle, or straight-ahead position.

Kicking the underside of the ball gives you a lot more height. Kicking toward the center of the ball will give you a low-line drive. Kicking the ball above the center will give you a ground ball with top spin.

Work at timing your kicks. Work for accuracy in the direction you want the ball to travel.

Spend time practicing kicking with *both* the left and right foot.

Spend most of your time learning how to use your instep for the different kicks.

Increase the speed of your approach and get your body weight into the kick to increase the power.

KICKING DRILLS

Without a Ball

1. Go through the kicking motions for the different soccer kicks. Check for correct foot action and for weight on the opposite foot. Look at yourself in a mirror if one is available. Have a partner check your form.
2. *Pretend* you are going after a ball rolling away from you. Catch up to it and make a nice instep kick on the run. Try this with an imaginary ball coming toward you from the front. Now make the kick with the ball coming to you from the right or left side. Keep your eye on the imaginary ball. Be sure to practice kicking with each foot.

With a Ball

1. Locate a wall that has no windows, or any fenced-in area. Place a ball one or two steps away from you but

near the wall or fence. Now, start practicing the different kicks, aiming the ball toward the wall or fence. Practice with a partner.

2. With one or more partners, practice by having one partner roll the ball slowly toward you. Step toward the ball and make your favorite kick in the direction of the wall or fence. Have the ball rolled toward your left or right side. The partner rolling the ball should move away quickly from the direction the ball is aimed.
3. Get a sturdy piece of cloth or netting and wrap it tightly around the ball. Attach one end of a piece of strong twine or rope to the cloth. Throw the other end of the rope over the crossbar portion of a baseball batter's cage or over the limb of a tree. Lower the ball so it is just touching the ground and secure the rope. Practice the different kicks. Raise the ball to anywhere from below the knee to waist height. Practice the volley kick.
4. After every kick, practice getting yourself free, and then move into an open area ready to receive a pass or defend against an opponent.

SHOOTING AT GOAL

It's a thrill to make a perfect shot at the goal! *Shooting* is forcing the ball toward the goal net for a possible score in any way the rules will allow.

Shooting at the goal for a score can be done with a kick while the ball is on the ground or in the air (volley position). Shots may also occur when the ball is in the air by using your knee, thigh, chest, or head. The most popular shots are made with the foot or forehead. At first, spend most of your time shooting using the instep kicks. You will learn how to meet the ball with the use of other parts of your body later. Learn and practice one kind of skill at a time. You will find later that this plan will make it much easier for you to put all the different skills together when game time approaches.

QUALIFICATIONS OF A SHOOTER

What kind of players make successful shooters? Usually they are alert and quick on their feet. They know the actions or moves of their teammates and the defenders. Above all, they are able to get themselves free in front of the goal so they can make a good shot. The following are some other qualifications and duties of good shooters:

1. They know how to make accurate shots at the goal.
2. They know how to work well with teammates who pass the ball to them for a quick shot.
3. They are agile, shifty dribblers who can dodge a defender standing in the path of the goal.
4. They are capable dribblers who can keep the ball moving near their feet.
5. They have the ability to trap the ball and then dribble into position to make a shot.
6. They are able to move in quickly toward the goal to meet the ball and shoot without trapping it.
7. They can make tackling plays, taking the ball from an opponent and quickly turn it into a shooting play.
8. They know how to anticipate a play to gain valuable time in beating a defender to the ball.
9. They know how to move toward a pass and keep their bodies between the ball and a defender.

Quite a list of duties and skills, isn't it? Don't be discouraged. Start practicing now and have fun as you go along.

A SHOOTER IN ACTION

You have learned that there are several ways to shoot the ball at the goal for a score. Let's discuss one way a shooter goes into action.

Your team has moved the ball into your opponent's half of the field. The ball has been brought close to the *shooting range* of the goal. You are the shooter, but the ball has not come into your possession yet.

1. After dodging a defender, you run swiftly into a clear position in front of the goal area.
2. Your teammate has dribbled free of another defender and makes a quick, accurate pass, sending the ball directly toward your right side.
3. You dart slightly to the right to meet the rolling ground ball. You trap it and get it quickly into position for a perfect right foot instep kick shot. The ball zooms past the goalkeeper and into the goal net for a score.

This is known as good timing and teamwork. You also remembered to:

1. Keep moving until you were free to receive a pass near the goal.
2. Keep your eyes on the ball.
3. Get your body weight moving in the direction of the ball once it was under control.
4. Get into position to use the instep kick for a shot that gave you greater power, speed, and accuracy.

HELPFUL HINTS

Learn to time your movements with those of your passing partners, so your body is moving toward the goal as you strike the ball on the run for a shot.

When in front of the net without the ball, do not stand still and allow a defender to block a pass from a teammate. Try to shift position to give your teammate a clear target for the pass to you.

If you are approaching the goal at an angle, it is a good idea to aim the ball at the far goal post when taking the shot.

As you position yourself for the shot, try to keep the goal in your line of vision.

SHOOTING DRILLS

1. Place the ball about seven-to-ten yards in front of a goal, net, backboard, or wall. Stand five yards behind the ball. Run up to the ball, put the nonkicking foot down the correct distance away from the ball and strike the ball with a smooth, instep shot at your target.
   a. Try runs to the ball from your left side, then from your right side.
   b. Try kicks with the right foot and then with the left foot.
2. From 20 yards, roll the ball forward but slowly sideways at the same time. Run up and kick the ball before it goes ten yards. Try doing this to the other side, using the other foot.
3. From 20 yards in front of the target, toss the ball into the air. Let it bounce on the ground. Pick a good bounce and *just before* it touches the ground, kick the ball with a *nice instep kick.* Be careful not to let the ball hit your toe. Get your knee over the ball for a low shot.
4. Have a partner toss the ball over your head. Run to the ball and take a nice volley shot toward your target with an instep kick.

4
Dribbling and Passing

An offensive player is moving the ball toward the goal. A defender is approaching to stop the advance. The player with the ball challenges the defender with a *body fake* to the left, and with a light *foot tap* s/he changes direction dribbling the ball to the right. The offensive player is again in the clear and continues to control the ball with short dribbles. Suddenly s/he makes an accurate pass to a teammate who is free closer to the goal area.

Many fans, players, and coaches agree that dribbling is the most artistic and exciting of all soccer skills. Learn all you can about the *dribbling and passing game.* Let's start with dribbling first.

DRIBBLING

Dribbling is moving the ball along the ground with short, gentle foot taps, pushes, or flicks. It is *ball control on the run,* with the dribbles made to move the ball forward, sideways, or even backward.

QUALIFICATIONS OF THE DRIBBLER

What kind of players make successful dribblers? They are in condition, alert, and able to think quickly. They are nimble, fast on their feet, and respected by their teammates. Above all, they must be able to stay calm when things are not going well. They must also be able to:

1. Dribble to the left, right, forward, or backward.
2. Keep possession and control of the ball while dribbling.
3. Dribble equally well with either foot.
4. Perform *change-of-direction* and *change-of-pace* running, with sudden stops and starts.
5. Use fake and trick moves to fool opponents.
6. Use the body as a *screen* when an opponent is trying to take the ball away.
7. Keep an eye on the ball and yet know what is going on elsewhere by quick glances.
8. Pass to a teammate quickly after a dribble.

Quite a list of qualifications, isn't it? Start practicing now. Learn to control the ball with your feet. Make quick passes to a teammate after dribbling on the run.

KNOWING WHEN TO DRIBBLE

It is smart to know when to dribble. Many beginning players dribble too long and allow opposing players to take the ball away from them. Here are some simple rules to remember:

1. Use the dribble if no opponent is near.
2. Dribble to get by an opponent if no teammate is near to receive a pass.
3. Dribble until an opponent is drawn out of position, then quickly pass to a teammate.
4. Use the dribble to surprise the opponent and set up a scoring play.

DIFFERENT KINDS OF DRIBBLING

The most popular ways to dribble are:
1. Inside-of-the-foot dribble.
2. Outside-of-the-foot dribble.

INSIDE OF THE FOOT DRIBBLE

The *inside of the foot* dribble is used most often to keep the ball directly in front of you and under control. It prevents an opposing player from trying to take the ball away from you.

Approaching the ball

1. Take short steps toward the ball.
2. The foot that is not dribbling should land slightly behind and to the side of the ball.
3. Start moving your body forward with your head extending over the ball.

The Dribbling

1. Your eyes are on the ball with your head and body still over the ball.
2. The *dribbling foot is pointed slightly outward* ready to move forward toward the ball. The knee is bent.
3. The weight is on the foot not dribbling.
4. *Begin* to touch, tap, coax, or push the ball gently forward along the ground about one to two feet with your dribbling foot. The foot is kept only about two or three inches off the ground when the ball is contacted with the front part of the *inside* (big toe) *of the foot. This completes the first dribble.*
5. As the weight shifts onto the first dribbling foot, start to make the *second dribble* with the other foot in the same way.

INSIDE-OF-FOOT DRIBBLE

The dribbling continues by contacting the ball lightly with each forward step. Shift from the right foot to the left foot until you see an opportunity to make a quick pass to an open teammate. You must remember that the inside-of-the-foot dribble requires that you keep the ball in front of you at all times. This helps you to be ready to control and protect the ball instantly from an oncoming opponent.

OUTSIDE OF THE FOOT DRIBBLE

The *outside of the foot* dribble is used mostly for fast running in an open field with no opponents nearby and no teammate open for a pass.

Approaching the ball

1. Get to the ball quickly.

2. Land the foot not dribbling about half-step back along side of the ball.
3. Body moves forward with eyes on the ball.

The Dribbling

1. Your eyes are on the ball.
2. The dribbling *foot is turned inward* ready to move forward to contact the ball. Your knee is bent.
3. Your weight is on the foot not dribbling.
4. Start tapping or pushing the ball straight forward along the ground about one to two feet. The dribbling foot is two or three inches off the ground as the front part of the *outside* (little toe) *of the foot* contacts the ball. *The first dribble is complete.*
5. After the dribble, you step down quickly on the dribbling foot, take another step with the other foot, and reach again to make the dribble with the original dribbling foot. You continue to contact the ball for the dribble with the same foot with every second step. *For example*: Push the ball with the right foot, then step right and step left; again push with the right foot and step right and step left. Repeat the action until you are ready to pass to a teammate.

MORE DRIBBLING SKILLS

Two additional skills a dribbler should learn are *feinting*, or faking, and *screening.*

Feinting while dribbling means getting past an opposing tackler by using all kinds of body, head, and feet movements, as well as change-of-direction and pace running. After a successful feinting, the dribbler must continue to watch for other opponents and teammates while at the same time keeping control of the ball.

OUTSIDE-OF-FOOT DRIBBLE

For a single feint:

1. Pretend you are about to dribble in one direction by shifting from one foot to the other by moving the head or body in that direction.
2. As your opponent begins to move in the fake direction of the dribble, quickly move in the opposite direction and begin your dribbling or pass to an open teammate.

For a double feint:

1. Make a move in the same way as in the single feint.
2. Your opponent this time does not move in the first direction because s/he was not fooled.
3. Quickly fake another dribble by making your *second action* a move in the opposite direction.

SINGLE FEINT DRIBBLE

1) FEINT LEFT

2) READY

3) DRIBBLE RIGHT

4. As your opponent starts to move toward the second fake direction, rapidly move in the direction away from him/her and begin your dribbling or pass to an open teammate.

Study and practice these skills just like the other aspects of the game. They will help you experience success. But more important, it's much more fun when you can outsmart an opponent. Another good soccer action you will want to learn is *screening.*

Screening while dribbling means protecting the ball by suddenly placing your body between the ball and the opponent tackler. This may happen after you have started to dribble and an opponent advances toward you to try to take the ball away. To protect and keep possession of the ball:

1. Make a quick screen by turning your body sideways so the ball is to one side or in front of you and the opposing tackler is on the opposite side or in back of you.
2. Keep shifting your feet to protect the ball while your side or back is toward your opponent.
3. Be sure you are always close to and playing the ball and not pushing your opponent.
4. Keep your eyes on the ball and watch for a quick get-away dribble or pass to a teammate.

That's all there is to it. It's tricky, exciting, and fun to work a fast screen on your opponents.

HELPFUL HINTS

Never overuse a dribble when you can pass to advance the ball toward the goal.

Keep inside-of-the-foot dribbles short.

Use the outside-of-the-foot dribble when you have an open field and want speed.

DOUBLE FEINT DRIBBLE
1) FEINT RIGHT
2) FEINT LEFT
3) DRIBBLE RIGHT

SCREENING WHILE DRIBBLING

Change to an inside-of-the-foot dribble when opponents appear nearby.
Know how and when to make a change of direction dribble or dribble forward with speed.
Feint by using a *shrug of the shoulders* or a *shuffle of the feet* to force an opponent to move in the wrong direction.
Play to protect the ball once you are forced to stop dribbling and can't locate a teammate free nearby.

DRILLS TO IMPROVE DRIBBLING

1. *Change of direction shuffle* (without the ball)
   a. Step to the left and slightly forward with your left foot.

b. Bring your right foot up to meet your left foot, shifting your weight to the right foot.

c. Step again with left foot, shifting your weight to the left foot.

d. Step to your right and move slightly forward with your right foot, putting your weight onto that foot.

e. Slide the left foot to the right foot, shifting your weight onto the left foot.

f. Step right with the right foot, shifting your weight onto the right foot.

Repeat this same drill from the beginning. But this time speed up your shifting by making a hopping motion instead of a stepping motion when you are changing direction. This *shuffle* can be practiced by running between markers placed on the ground.

2. *Feinting practice*

   a. Place a ball in front of you and make believe you are going to dribble to your left. Then suddenly push or tap the ball softly to the right with the outside of your right foot.

   b. Practice the same drill but feint to the right and make a quick dribble to your left.

   c. Make up your own feinting drills with double fake moves before actually touching the ball for a dribble.

3. *Dribbling between markers.* Use chairs, cardboard, or bundles of paper for markers and place them on a smooth outdoor or indoor area. Space the markers equally. Start dribbling between and around each marker by making use of the different feints and dribbling plays.

4. *One-on-one.* Get a partner to act as a defensive player. Mark two boundary lines about five yards apart. Place a ball in front of you about ten yards from the defensive player. Start your slow dribbling and try to move around and beyond your defensive player. You must stay between the five-yard markers. Make use of your feints, stops, and screening plays.

PASSING

The passing game in soccer calls for teamwork among the eleven players. No one player can do much alone to get the ball into a scoring position. Each player must know how to share the ball. The best and safest way to share the ball and try for scoring plays is by use of the pass.

Passing is moving the ball *with accuracy* to a teammate, or receiver. The most popular passes in soccer are made with the foot. Passing is often the link between players acting as a team. The most widely used passes with the foot are:

1. Inside-of-the-foot push pass.
2. Outside-of-the-foot flick pass.
3. Inside-of-the-foot lob pass.
4. Heel pass (very rarely used).
5. Sole-of-the-foot pass.

INSIDE-OF-THE-FOOT PASS

This is the most accurate pass in soccer. It is made on the ground and should be a short pass. Practice it more often than the others.

1. Approach the ball with the foot that will remain on

INSIDE FOOT PUSH-PASS

the ground slightly behind and to the side of the ball. Shift your weight to this foot.

2. Just before the other foot contacts the ball for the pass start turning your hips and shoulder a little away from the direction of the pass.
3. The passing leg is slightly bent at the knee, with the foot turned outward a few inches off the ground.
4. The body is over the ball.
5. Have the passing leg start an easy sweeping motion from the hip, contacting the ball with the inside of the foot between the big toe and the heel for a smooth push pass to your teammate.
6. After contacting the ball, make a good follow-through with the inside of the foot moving in the direction of the passing target. Move quickly to a

free position on the field ready to receive a pass from one of your teammates.

OUTSIDE-OF-THE-FOOT FLICK PASS

This pass is usually made while dribbling. The ball is contacted with the outside of the foot near the little toe area. A short pass to the side is made with a little outward flick or push at the ball.

1. Approach the ball and place your ground foot a little behind and to the side of it. Keep your weight on this foot.
2. Your body is behind the ball, with the passing foot a few inches off the ground. The knee is bent.
3. Reach to contact the ball with the outside of the foot near the little toe area.
4. With an outward flick of the foot, you send a short pass to the side to a teammate.
5. The follow-through is made by straightening your passing leg, adding a little hip and knee action in the direction of the passing target.
6. Immediately after a short follow-through, your weight is shifted to the passing foot, while continuing your running stride.

INSIDE-OF-THE-FOOT LOB PASS

This pass is made to clear the ball over the head of an opponent who is in the path of where you want the pass to go. It is made while the ball is coming to you on the fly or on the bounce.

1. Quickly approach the spot where you feel the ball will land. Have the side of the ground foot slightly facing the oncoming fly or bouncing ball.

2. Balance on the ground foot and start raising your passing foot with the inside of that foot toward the ball, toes pointed outward.
3. Strike the ball with the inside of the foot while you start to lean in the opposite direction from the pass. Leaning will help you maintain your balance.
4. A follow-through is made with a sharp knee action that helps to send the ball away with power and accuracy.

In *lob* passing, the higher off the ground the ball is contacted, the higher the ball will go. This means you must decide and prepare yourself to meet the ball at the best height to get off the kind of pass you need to reach your receiver.

HEEL AND SOLE-OF-THE-FOOT PASSES

Each of these passes is usually made while dribbling. They are short, backward passes that can fool an opponent. On completing one of these passes, move quickly to an open spot to receive a return pass.

The *heel pass* is made by hitting or pushing the ball backward to a teammate with the use of the heel. The ground foot is slightly to the side and about even with the ball. The passing foot steps directly over the ball before hitting, striking, or pushing it with the heel for a *backward pass* to a teammate. Continue the follow-through by leaning forward after kicking the ball backward.

The *sole-of-the-foot pass* is also a backward pass. The difference is that this pass is made by contacting the ball with the sole of the foot. Get the ground foot slightly to the side and behind the ball. Start by placing the sole of the passing foot *lightly* on the ball. With a quick leg-foot move, roll or pull the ball backward to a teammate

FLICK PASS

behind you. You should be leaning forward on the follow-through, ready to move into an open area to receive a pass.

HELPFUL HINTS

Have a picture in your mind of the location of your teammates and opponents before making a pass.

After completing a pass, move quickly into a free position ready to receive a pass.

Work for short, accurate passes before trying the long passes.

Keep opponents guessing until you are ready to make a pass.

Make your passes just hard enough so your teammates can control the ball.

When teammates are running full speed, aim your

1) MEETING THE BALL 2) PASS FOLLOW-THROUGH
INSIDE FOOT VOLLEY PASS

pass so it will travel just in front of them to an open spot.

PASSING DRILLS

1. With Partner. Find a smooth outdoor or indoor area. Place a ball in front of you. Have your partner stand about ten feet to your left. Start to dribble forward slowly and make a short *inside of the right foot pass* to your partner on the left. Your partner now traps the ball on a slow run and makes a short *outside of the right foot pass* back to you. Continue this dribbling forward, passing to one another until you reach the end of the playing area.

a. Switch positions so you will make the outside-of-the-foot passes and your partner the inside-of-the-foot passes.

b. Start to speed up your dribbling and passing.

c. Try the same passes to one another from a greater distance apart.

d. Practice touching the ball only once for a dribble, then make a pass. Try touching the ball several times to dribble and pass.

Work hard, but make your practice drills fun!

2. Two Against One. Have a partner stand to one side of you about ten yards away. Let another player act as a defensive player by standing about ten yards in front of you and your partner. Place a ball on the ground in front of you.

a. You and your partner dribble forward carefully and try to make a pass around and beyond the defensive player. *You must make the dribbles and passes between two sideline markers, which are no more than ten yards apart.*

b. Change positions until each player has had the opportunity to play defense.

c. Shorten or lengthen the sideline markers depending upon your experience.

5
Trapping the Ball

Receiving the ball! Trapping the ball! Controlling the ball! These are skills you will hear fans and coaches discuss when praising or grading a player's ability to get possession of a rolling, bouncing, or fly ball. Such players are known as *masters of the ball.* They can stop and control a ball that is traveling toward them from any direction without the use of their hands. They treat and trap the ball gently, swiftly, and accurately with their feet, thighs, chest, stomach, and head. *Trapping* is a way of bringing a moving ball under control.

REQUIREMENTS FOR TRAPPING

There are certain rules to remember when you are about to trap a ball.

1. Decide quickly which is the best trapping skill to use for a rolling, bouncing, or fly ball coming toward you.
2. Always try to use the softest parts of your body for trapping a bouncing or fly ball. The chest, stomach, or thighs are best.
3. Know how to slow up and trap a swift ball the instant it makes contact with your body.

4. Keep your eyes on the ball as it contacts your body and immediately thereafter.
5. Keep your body balanced throughout the trap play.
6. Know immediately what to do with the ball after making a successful trap play.

An Extra Special Skill. There is one part of trapping that all soccer players must learn early. It's the ability to stop or slow up a swiftly traveling ball yet not have it bounce off too far from your body. To do this you must move the part of the body that makes contact with the ball *in the same direction* the ball is traveling. This area of the body gives or draws back slightly the instant the ball makes contact with it. This is known as *cushioning* and it makes it easier to trap the ball for better control. It's like catching a hard baseball without a glove, where you must give or draw your hand back to prevent stinging which may make you drop the ball on contact.

THE DIFFERENT TRAP PLAYS

The most widely used trapping skills are:

1. For a rolling ball
   a. Sole of the foot.
   b. Inside of the foot.
   c. Outside of the foot.
2. For a bouncing or fly ball
   a. Sole of the foot.
   b. Inside of the foot.
   c. Outside of the foot.
   d. Thigh or leg.
   e. Chest or stomach.
   f. Instep of the foot.

ROLLING SOLE-OF-FOOT

ROLLING BALL, SOLE-OF-THE-FOOT TRAP

This trap is used mainly when a ball is rolling in your direction.

1. Move in front of the ball that is coming toward you, and keep your eyes on it.
2. Place the foot *not* trapping the ball slightly behind and to the side of the ball. Keep your weight on this leg and bend the knee a little.
3. The trapping foot begins to reach out with the toes pointing up and the heel down a few inches above the ground. The knee is slightly bent.
4. Suddenly squeeze or wedge the ball between the sole of your foot and the ground for a trap, while your head moves forward and your weight is on the other foot.
5. Control the ball and get ready to pass quickly, dribble, or shoot for a goal.

ROLLING BALL, INSIDE-OF-THE-FOOT TRAP

This trap is often used by players who wish to trap and pass in almost one motion. It is also used when the ball is coming at the player from an angle or the side.

1. Turn so the outside part of your body and the foot you are not using for trapping are facing the ball that is coming at you.
2. The foot you are using for the trapping is farther from the ball.
3. Shift your weight onto the foot nearest the oncoming ball, and lean in the direction of the ball.
4. Bend the knee of your trapping leg toward the ball, and raise the foot a few inches from the ground with the toes pointed outward.

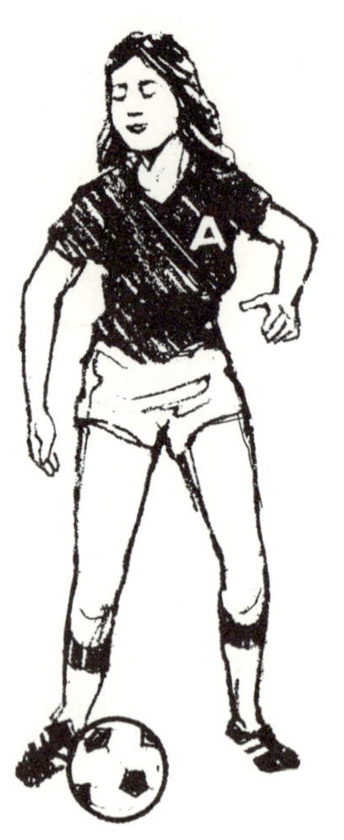

ROLLING INSIDE-OF-FOOT TRAP

ROLLING OUTSIDE-OF-FOOT TRAP

5. Trap the ball with the full *inside area of the foot.* Make sure to give in the direction the ball is traveling. Then pivot quickly, changing your foot movement in the direction you want to send the ball.

ROLLING BALL, OUTSIDE-OF-THE-FOOT TRAP

This trap is a little more difficult to master. Do not get discouraged if you can't do it well at first. It is most useful when the trapper wants to move or pivot quickly in any direction with the ball.

1. Approach the oncoming ball so your trapping foot will be in position to make an *outside of the foot* play.
2. Shift your weight onto the foot *not* doing the trapping. Keep your eyes on the ball, with your arms held slightly outward for balance.
3. Lift the trapping foot a few inches off the ground, with the knee bent facing the ball. Then stop, or trap, the ball between the *outside portion of the foot* and the ground. Remember to give or draw back a little with the foot in the direction the ball is traveling to prevent it from bouncing away from you.
4. To get the ball going in another direction without stopping it is a different skill. Get the ball to meet the outside of the foot just long enough to *slow it down* while you pivot and turn your body in the direction you want the ball to go.

Learn and practice these important trap plays. They will help you to control and make the ball do what you want. These are easier to learn than the fly or bouncing ball trap skills. In the fly or bouncing ball trap plays, the trapper must always make a quick decision whether to trap the ball while it is in the air or immediately upon its touching the ground.

BOUNCING BALL SOLE-OF-FOOT TRAP

BOUNCING BALL, SOLE-OF-THE-FOOT TRAP

This trap play is much the same as the rolling ball trap.

1. Quickly move into a position so that the ball will land in front of you.
2. Stretch the trapping leg forward, but bend the knee very slightly. Trap the ball immediately after it lands with a relaxed (not stiff) ankle between the *sole of the foot* and the ground.
3. Keep your weight on the other foot and your eyes on the ball, holding your arms slightly away from your body for balance.

BOUNCING BALL, INSIDE-OF-THE-FOOT TRAP

This trap play is also much the same as the rolling ball trap.

FLYBALL INSIDE-OF-FOOT TRAP

1. Lean the side of your body and foot not trapping in the direction of the ball coming toward you.
2. Shift your weight onto the foot nearest the ball while you keep your eyes on the ball.
3. Lift your trapping foot from the ground with your knee bent toward the oncoming ball and your toes pointed outward.
4. Trap the ball with the *inside of the foot* and be sure to give way in the direction the ball is traveling.

BOUNCING BALL, OUTSIDE-OF-THE-FOOT TRAP

This is a very difficult trap to learn. The routine is much the same as in the rolling ball trap. If you or your teacher or coach feel you are ready to spend time on practicing this skill, then do so. Otherwise, stick to the other skills you know best.

FLYBALL THIGH TRAP

1. Get into position so the trapping side of your body and foot is leaning in the direction from which the ball is approaching.
2. Shift your weight onto the foot not doing the trapping. Bend your knee and keep your eyes on the ball.
3. Lift your trapping foot in front of you with the outside of the foot facing the oncoming ball.
4. Trap the ball between the outside of the foot and the ground. Get ready to pivot in the direction you want to go with the ball.

FLY BALL, THIGH (LEG) TRAP

This trap is useful when fly or high bouncing balls are dropped straight down toward you, or when they are coming at you at an angle.

1. Get into position to meet the fly ball coming at you just about waist height from the side.
2. Turn your body slightly toward the oncoming ball, with your weight shifting to the sole of the foot not trapping the ball. Bend the knee of this leg slightly and keep your eyes on the ball.
3. Get the trapping foot off the ground with the knee bent just about waist height and the foot hanging loosely.
4. Move the hanging foot slightly closer to the oncoming ball than the knee, and meet the ball for the trap with the soft, fleshy part of the *inside portion of the thigh.*
5. Move the leg in the direction the ball is moving and let the ball drop softly in front of you. Hold your arms out for balance.

To trap a ball dropping straight down in front of you, move the thigh up, let the ball hit the *top of the thigh,* and drop the leg quickly. The rest of the action is the same.

CHEST AND STOMACH TRAPS

These traps are used when the ball comes toward you at about the neck, chest, or stomach height. The ball may be traveling toward you on a bounce or fly.

Chest Trap. If the fly ball is above chest height and dropping down toward you:

1. Get your body directly in position under the place where the ball is about to drop.
2. Spread your feet about a shoulder's width apart, bend your knees slightly, and place one foot slightly ahead of the other.
3. Start *leaning backward a little* from the knees to the

1) BALL LANDING

2) GROUND DROP FOR CONTROL

shoulders, with your chest directly under the spot where the ball will land.

4. Let the ball drop softly onto your chest area and move slightly downward as the ball makes contact. This forms a cushion for the trap.
5. Quickly straighten your body and let the ball drop near you for quick control. Keep your hands out for body balance and to keep them from touching the ball.

Chest Trap (Girls). The girl's chest trap is done a little differently than the boy's. The difference is that *girls are allowed to cross their arms over their chests before the ball makes contact.* All other movements are the same.

GIRL'S CHEST TRAP

If the ball comes toward you *chest-high from a swift bounce,* get directly in front of the ball. Keep your feet spread apart. The instant the ball contacts you draw in or suck in your stomach or chest. Keep your shoulders and head over the ball and let it drop in front of you for control.

Stomach Trap. If a hard hit ball is coming at you on the fly or on a bounce at stomach height:

1. Get your body directly in the path of the ball and spread your feet apart.
2. Start *leaning toward* the oncoming ball.
3. The instant the ball meets the stomach area, draw in your stomach as if you were going to take a deep breath. Get up on your toes as soon as the ball makes contact to make a cushion for the ball.

BOUNCING BALL STOMACH TRAP

4. Trap the ball and let it drop lightly in front of you for control.

HELPFUL HINTS

Think about getting the ball under control before you try to dribble, pass, or shoot.
Learn to trap and control the ball with either foot.
Spend your time on the more popular trap plays and not on the head and shoulder traps, unless your teacher or coach thinks you are ready for them.
Don't stand flatfooted waiting for the ball to reach you.
Always move swiftly into the best position for the trap play you decide to make.
When trapping, think of your control, never letting

the ball bounce away from you and into an opponent's control.

TRAPPING DRILLS

1. Have a partner roll the ball toward you. To stop the ball, use a:
   a. Sole of the foot trap.
   b. Inside of the right foot trap.
   c. Inside of the left foot trap.
   d. Outside of the right foot trap.
   e. Outside of the left foot trap.

   Switch with your partner and roll the ball toward him or her.
2. Toss a ball into the air and use a:
   a. Top of the thigh trap.
   b. Instep of the foot trap.
   c. Inside of the foot trap.
   d. Outside of the foot trap.
   e. Chest trap.
   f. Head trap.
3. Have a partner toss the ball toward you from a distance. Try all the different types of traps. Do the same for your partner.

Practice until you can trap the ball using either your left or right foot.

6
Heading the Ball

It has been reported that some soccer players show greater skills than others in "kicking with the head." What was really meant was that these players were *heading the ball*, or using a part of the forehead to make a play. *Heading* means that a fly or bouncing ball traveling toward you is played by contacting it with the *forehead.*

There are many times during a game when the soccer ball is in the air and beyond the reach of a player's feet. It is then that heading plays become useful and fun. Fans especially enjoy a play where one player sends a fly ball pass to a teammate who then makes a *forehead shot* at the goal for a score.

Other fans appreciate a smart *defensive heading play.* This happens when an offensive player places a swift, high shot at the goal just below the crossbar to make what looks like a sure goal. Then out of nowhere comes a defensive player who lunges high into the air to meet the ball with the forehead and prevents a score.

MAKE USE OF THE HEADING GAME

It's good to know that heading plays are used on both offense and defense. The different ways to use them are:

1. Passing to a teammate.
2. Heading and trapping the ball in front of you for quick control.
3. Shooting at the goal.
4. Heading, or clearing, the ball away from your goal area and out of danger.

Players learn to direct a header play to the left, right, forward, or backward. They can meet the ball from a standing, running, jumping, leaping, lunging, or even a diving position.

SAFETY HINTS

Meeting the ball with the forehead is a beautiful play to watch in a soccer game. In most other sports, players are taught to catch, strike, hit, or dodge the ball that travels toward the head. In soccer you are taught to use the forehead as a weapon. But there are certain rules that a young player must learn before practicing these plays.

1. Do not strike the ball with the top, sides, or back of the head. And, of course, try to keep the ball from hitting your face, ears, or jaw.
2. Do not try to head a ball that is below the shoulders. An opponent at the same time may try for a kicking play and accidentally strike your face.
3. Always strike the ball with the middle of your forehead. This is the strongest part of the skull.
4. Do not close your eyes when the ball is coming at your head. Give the ball a safe, solid target. Follow the path of the ball until it contacts your forehead. You may have to blink momentarily, but open your

eyes quickly and follow the flight of the ball after contact.

THE DIFFERENT HEADING PLAYS

These are heading plays you should practice.

1. Heading ball with feet on ground.
2. Heading ball from a jump.
3. Heading ball to side.
4. Heading ball to feet.
5. Heading ball to rear (backheading).

HEADING BALL WITH FEET ON GROUND

A fly ball is coming down near your area.

1. Face the ball and get directly under it. Always keep your eyes on the ball.
2. Spread your feet in a solid, comfortable position, with your knees slightly bent.
3. Move your trunk (upper body) backward from the waist. Your eyes continue to follow the ball while your forehead is facing upward.
4. Just before the ball is about to contact the center portion of your forehead, tighten, or stiffen, your neck muscles.
5. Quickly move your trunk and head forward. Hit the ball with your forehead toward the spot you have chosen. This takes perfect timing.
6. The trunk and head move forward slightly on the follow-through.

Try hitting the ball with a driving motion of the trunk and a snap of the head in the direction you want the ball to travel. Then immediately move into position for the next play.

1) LEANING BACK, EYE ON BALL

2) FORWARD HEAD STRIKE

FEET ON GROUND HEADING

HEADING BALL FROM A JUMP

This heading play takes good timing to meet the ball at the peak or height of the jump. You must leap and reach higher than your opponent who is also jumping for the ball. A player must be careful not to foul an opponent by jumping into him or her while heading the ball on the run.

1. Get in position directly under the oncoming ball. Keep your eyes on the ball throughout the action.
2. Start your jump upward by driving off one foot. You should reach your peak height just as the ball is about to contact the forehead.
3. Your arms are slightly bent at the elbow, with the hands raised forward at about chest height for balance.
4. Your trunk and head are back and your feet are off the ground with knees bent forward.
5. Meet the ball with the forehead and at the same time snap the trunk and head forward, sending the ball to the planned target.
6. Follow through with your head facing the ball. Land on your feet, ready for play.

HEADING BALL TO SIDE

Oftentimes a player finds that the safest way to keep control of the ball is to make a head pass to the right or left to a teammate who is free when all the other teammates are well guarded by the opposing players. It's also possible that the only way to make a goal on certain plays is to use a *side header* shot. In still another situation you may be forced to stop an opponent from scoring by *heading the ball to the side.*

These side heading plays are done in almost the same way as the *feet on the ground* and *jump heading* plays. The big difference in heading the ball sideways is in

HEADING BALL FROM JUMP

meeting the ball. You must twist your body and turn your head toward the side you want the ball to go. Then you hit the ball slightly to the side of the forehead and follow through with your head facing in the direction the ball is traveling.

HEADING BALL TO FEET

This play is also used when players want to keep control of the ball. Other players may choose to pass the ball to a nearby teammate's feet. The skills for heading this kind of play are:

1. Get under the ball as you did for the other plays.
2. Let the ball drop down in front of your face just a

1) BALL MEETS FRONT-SIDE OF FOREHEAD

2) SHARP HEAD TWIST TO SIDE

JUMP-HEADING BALL TO SIDE

little lower than your head. Your eyes stay on the ball, and your knees are slightly bent and the heels are off the ground.

3. Lean forward and downward with your upper body and head. Pull in your chin and nudge the ball with your forehead so it lands at your feet or at a nearby teammate's feet.
4. Follow the flight of the ball while your upper body is leaning slightly forward. Be ready to move into position for the next play.

HEADING BALL TO REAR (Backheading)

There are times when heading a ball forward or sideways is not safe because your opponents are guarding these areas. This means you should make a head pass to a teammate located behind you. This play is often called *backheading* because you are using your forehead to make a pass to the rear. This play is made from a standing or jumping position.

When in a *standing position*, get in front of the oncoming ball. Spread your feet solidly on the ground with the knees bent. Your arms should be forward and

1) READY STANCE FOR BALL CONTACT 2) STRIKING BALL BACKWARDS

BACKHEADING

slightly outward for balance. Your upper body and head are in a ready position. Just as the ball is about to land on your forehead, start bending your trunk and head backward. With a quick burst, straighten your knees and shove your hips forward. At the same time try to push your shoulders and head backward again while hitting the ball with the upper part of the forehead. Your back ends up in a temporarily arched position. Recover your balance and get ready for the next play.

For the *jumping play* you must leap up to meet the ball. Everything else is the same, but the timing for meeting the ball with the forehead is more difficult. You must also land safely on your feet after heading the ball.

Heading the ball can be lots of fun whether in practice or in a real game situation. Many younger and older players try heading the ball as an everyday exercise. The skills will appear difficult at first. Keep working on the simple heading plays from a standing position before spending time on the jumping skills.

HELPFUL HINTS

Practice the safety hints at the beginning of the chapter. Hitting the ball with the forehead just above the ball's center sends it downward more. Hitting the ball just below the center sends it upward more. Hitting the ball directly underneath sends it straight up.

Don't fear the ball. Let the forehead attack the ball with confidence.

Always get in a position to face the ball.

Head the ball for distance when your team wants it away from your goal area. Work for accuracy at all other times.

When an opponent is nearby, time your jump for the

ball just *before* s/he jumps. Be sure to jump straight into the air and not into your opponent.

HEADING DRILLS

1. How many times can you juggle the ball with your head? Five, ten, fifteen?
2. Stand three-to-four feet from a wall or backboard. How many times can you knock the ball against the wall with your head without touching the ball with your hands?
3. Toss a ball lightly toward your partner's head. Your partner then heads it back to your head. How many times can you keep the ball moving from head to head? Three, four, five?
4. Using a badminton or volleyball net, play a game of heading tennis. The ball must be headed over the net. The ball can touch the ground only once after it hits the feet or body.
5. Toss the ball into the air, run forward, jump, and meet the ball with the correct part of your head.

Pick a target nearby. Repeat the drill, hitting the ball toward the target.

7
Tackling and Charging, The Defensive Game

The offensive, or attacking, team is moving the ball closer to the opponent's goal. The defending players try to prevent a score. It's a battle of wits between the attackers and the defenders. An offensive player quickly finds an open field and is dribbling near the goal. But suddenly, out of nowhere, a defender catches up to the dribbler and, with quick footwork, captures the ball. A great play! A score was saved and the opposite team now has the ball. The fans appreciate the fine play. This kind of action is called smart tackling by the defensive player. It is not the same tackling you find in regular tackle football, however.

THE SOCCER TACKLE AND CHARGE

Tackling in soccer is a way of using the feet to take the ball away from the feet of an opponent. Every team needs well-drilled tacklers who use sharp footwork to keep their opponents from scoring. Some of the best defenders in soccer are called the wizards of the tackle.

Another part of tackling is called *shoulder charging.* A shoulder charge in soccer is done by a defender to force a dribbler away from the ball. The idea is for the defender to shove, block, or nudge the dribbler's shoulder area. *This kind of body contact and charging is not allowed in the girls' game.*

RULES FOR TACKLING AND CHARGING

Tackling and charging illegally in soccer can cause injuries to players. It is important that you learn the correct way to make these plays.

Legal tackles must be done from the front or side with the use of the feet and shoulder only. You cannot use your hands to push, hold, grab, or tackle the dribbler from behind. It is illegal to trip or to dive into the ball with both feet at the same time.

Legal charges are made when the defender's shoulder moves solidly into the shoulder of the offensive player. It is illegal to use the hands, elbows, or hips. The upper part of the arm must be held against the side of the body when your shoulder meets the dribbler's shoulder. You are not allowed to charge the dribbler in the back or chest.

You must learn these rules and practice them. You will be penalized if the referee feels that your tackling and blocking was dangerous or violent. A penalty means that your opponents will receive a free kick.

MAKING USE OF THE TACKLE

The reason for tackling is to take the ball away from your opponent. Tackling plays will force the dribbler:

1. To slow up or stop moving toward your goal. This gives your teammates extra time to organize a better defense.
2. To kick the ball out-of-bounds or away instead of to a teammate.
3. To make a bad pass.

4. To lose control of the ball to the tackler and put the dribbling team suddenly on defense.

THE DIFFERENT TACKLING PLAYS

These are the more popular tackling plays you should learn.

1. Front two-leg tackle.
2. Front one-leg tackle.
3. Tackling from the side.
4. Tackling when you approach from the rear.
5. Sole of the foot tackle.
6. Sliding tackle (illegal for girls' game).
7. Hook Tackle (illegal for girls' game).

THE DEFENSIVE STANCE

To make smart tackles you must be in an alert position or stance. Defensive players don't like to have dribblers go past them and move closer to the goal. You must make many fast moves to make successful tackles. The first thing you do is to move quickly into a position that puts you between the dribbler and the goal. This puts you in a position facing the dribbler and ready for the tackle.

1. Stand alert with your feet about shoulder-width apart. Your toes are pointed slightly outward with the weight evenly divided on them.
2. Bend the knees a little, and lean slightly forward into a crouch position.
3. Have your upper arms at your sides with the lower arms and hands pointed slightly outward and forward.
4. You are now in a ready position to move quickly in any direction to stop the forward progress of the dribbler.

A good stance puts you in a smart position to challenge

DEFENSIVE STANCE

the shifty dribbler with a number of fake moves. You may wish to back away a little and then move forward with a sudden burst of speed to make a tackle for the ball. Or you may fake a quick move forward, spin on the ball of your pivot foot, back away a step, and, with perfect timing, make a swift tackle to stop the dribbler. As you can see, soccer may often develop into a battle between a top dribbler and a smart tackler. A smart tackler will make his or her move for the ball immediately *after* the dribbler nudges the ball forward.

FRONT TWO-LEG TACKLE

This tackle is best used when you are directly in front and near the dribbler who has very little room to dodge you. *It is not allowed in the girls' game.*

1. Get into an alert stance position.
2. Quickly move forward and get both feet in front of

FRONT TWO-LEG TACKLE

the ball, moving first one foot to block then the other with the heels almost touching. The toes and knees are turned outward and you lean slightly forward. *It is illegal to step in front of the ball with both feet at the same time.*

3. Trap the ball between your feet while at the same time giving your opponent a slight shoulder charge. This charge will get your opponent off balance and force the dribbler away from the ball.
4. Make the tackle by stepping forward a little and to the side with one foot, while the other foot pulls the ball away from the dribbler.
5. If your charge is with the right shoulder, you should step away from the ball with the left foot. Follow through with a nice pull or drag of the ball so you are in a position to make a quick dribble or pass to a teammate.

FRONT ONE-LEG TACKLE

This tackle is best used from a position directly in front of your opponent or from a front angle position. It is used to force the dribbler to lose control of the ball to force a bad pass, or to stop his/her forward progress.

1. Take your defensive stance.
2. Wait for your opponent to start dribbling forward. Make a swift body lunge forward, placing the inside of your tackling foot solidly against the ball with the knee bent for better support.
3. Block or trap the ball with your tackling foot. Shift the weight onto your other foot, which is slightly back and to the side. Spread your legs apart just far enough to maintain good support and balance. The ball is now wedged between your foot and your opponent's foot.
4. Lean forward slightly.
5. You may have to make a shoulder charge at this point to help free the ball from your opponent. If you make a right foot tackle, you charge with the right shoulder. The left shoulder is used when you make a left foot tackle.
6. Start stepping forward or sideways with the other foot. Complete your tackle with a strong push, lift, or drag of the ball over the dribbler's foot.
7. After getting the ball, move quickly between the ball and your opponent.

TACKLING FROM THE SIDE

This tackle is mainly used when you cannot quite get your body completely in front of the dribbler.

1. Sprint until you catch up to the dribbler. You are now running shoulder-to-shoulder with your opponent.

FRONT ONE-LEG TACKLE

2. Try to get at least a half-step ahead of the dribbler and quickly make a pivot turn toward the ball using the foot closest to your opponent.
3. At the same time swing your other foot around to make a strong tackle at the very center of the ball. The weight is on the tackle foot with the knees bent and the body leaning over the ball.
4. After the ball is blocked, you make the same tackle moves as in the front one-leg tackle.

TACKLING FROM A REAR APPROACH

This tackle play is used when you must catch up to a dribbler who got past you or a dribbler who just received a pass and is well ahead of you.

1. Use your best sprinting speed to catch up to the dribbler. Look over the situation carefully and quickly.
2. Look for the right timing to make your next move for the tackle.
3. Get the foot nearest to your opponent planted firmly on the ground so it is pointing slightly toward the ball ready to start the pivot. Support your weight on this foot while the other foot and leg is set to block and tackle the ball.
4. You are suddenly in a ready position to complete the pivot turn inward while the other leg makes a forceful tackle swing to the ball.
5. The tackle is made by taking the ball off your opponent's foot. Follow through by putting yourself quickly between the ball and your opponent. You are now ready to pass or dribble the ball.

There are other styles of making a side or rear approach tackle. You must ask your coach about them.

A girl can make these tackles by running alongside the

TACKLE FROM REAR-SIDE

dribbler. With the outside portion of the foot closest to the dribbler, you shove, push, tap, or kick the ball away from the dribbler and toward a teammate. Or you may be in a position to control the ball yourself after the surprise tackle. If there is a lot of space between the ball and the dribbler, you can use the inside of your foot to tackle the ball and get free. Girls must be careful not to use body contact when trying these tackles. Boys may use contact, but both boys and girls should be careful not to trip or push the dribbler illegally.

SOLE-OF-THE-FOOT TACKLE

This tackle is not used as often as the others, but it is to your advantage to know how it works. It is similar to the sole-of-the-foot trap. It can be used when you can't get into position to make the other tackles.

1. Take your defensive stance in front of the dribbler.
2. As the dribbler taps the ball forward, make a quick step forward toward the ball with your tackling foot.
3. Have the sole of the tackling foot facing the ball with the toe pointing upward and the heel close to the ground.
4. Make your tackle by suddenly wedging the ball between the sole and the ground.
5. Be ready to protect the ball from your opponent with a push, tap, pass, or dribble.

SLIDING TACKLE

This tackle is used when all others are not possible. It is the very last chance the defender has to block or tackle the ball. The defender must be sure that the tackle foot touches the ball and not the dribbler's feet. This tackle is not allowed in the girls' game.

1. You are running across the field to catch up to the dribbler. Wait for the moment when the dribbler's leg nearest to you is out of contact with the ball.
2. Get ready to reach or shove your foot farthest from your opponent so it is aimed directly at the ball.
3. Start falling and sliding toward the ball by straightening and stretching the leg farthest from your opponent (tackling leg) and hit, push, kick the ball away hard from the dribbler. Use any part of the instep, sole, or toes of your foot to meet the ball. The opposite leg is bent and the knee with the foot pointed backwards. Make sure to break or lighten your fall to the ground with the use of your full arm and side.
4. Start sliding toward the ball by straightening and stretching your tackling leg, and hit, push, or kick the ball away hard from the dribbler. Use any part of the instep, sole, or toes of your feet to meet the ball.

You are not trying to get the ball yourself on this play. Your first duty is to try and force your opponent to lose the ball to the control of your teammate.

SLIDING HOOK TACKLE

This tackle is almost the same as for the regular side tackle for boys. The only difference is that you drop to the ground for the hook tackle instead of staying on your feet as in the side tackle. Also, in the regular sliding tackle you kick the ball away from the dribbler, but for this tackle you *try to keep control of the ball.* It is illegal for girls to use this tackle.

1. Get into your regular defensive stance as you face the dribbler who is in front and slightly to one side of you.

1) READY SLIDE FOR TACKLE

2) PUSH-KICK BALL AWAY

SLIDING TACKLE

2. Start sliding toward the ball with your tackling foot as you did for the regular sliding tackle.
3. Now keep the tackling knee slightly bent and facing the dribbler. The foot is raised a bit from the ground and the instep faces the ball.
4. Make a safe landing on the opposite leg, side, and hand.
5. Quickly block or hook the ball away from the dribbler with the instep of the foot.
6. Get back on your feet and keep control of the ball as the dribbler drives past you.

The sliding and hook tackles are difficult skills to learn. They take practice and must not be tried unless a teacher, coach, or other adult is helping you. Here are some extra hints and drills you can begin to learn and practice.

HELPFUL HINTS

For Charging:

Keep the arms and hands in close to your body when making a charge.

Try to aim high at your opponent's shoulder and make sure you use your shoulder to make contact.

Make sure both you and your opponent have one foot on the ground during the charge.

Do not hit, contact, or charge your opponent from the rear.

Charge when your opponent's weight is on the foot farthest from you.

Never charge your opponent violently.

For Tackling:

Study when and how to challenge the ball. Always be alert to a defender's stance. Be ready to shift in any direction but *never cross your feet* when forced to challenge a dribbler.

Start your tackles when the foot of a dribbler leaves contact with the ball. Do not start your tackle too soon or too far away from the ball.

Make fake movements with your body and head to confuse and fool the dribbler before making your real tackle.

Always try to take a defensive stance position between the goal and your opponent.

Do not try to tackle the ball too early when approaching the dribbler from behind. Wait for the right moment.

Always go for the ball, not your opponent, when tackling.

Learn to tackle with either foot. If the ball is closer to your left foot make the block with your left foot. The same with the right foot when the ball is on that side.

TACKLING DRILLS

1. Take your regular defensive tackle stance.
   a. Quickly shift to your right about the length of two sideways steps without crossing your feet.
   b. Shift to the left. Forward. Backward.
   c. Pretend you are tackling the ball from a dribbler. Try the tackle with your right foot, then with your left foot.
   d. Check your moves in front of a mirror.
2. Have a partner without the ball act as a dribbler. Take your defensive stance and pretend you are challenging the ball for a front one- and two-leg tackle and shoulder charge.
   a. Make these same moves with a real ball.
   b. Practice the tackling and shoulder charge from your right and left sides.

c. Trade positions with your partner. You act as the dribbler and your partner as the tackler.

3. Have a partner without the ball act as a dribbler.
   a. The dribbler gets past you.
   b. You catch up to the dribbler and pretend to make a side or rear tackle motion.
   c. Do the same drill with a real ball.
   d. Try these from both your right and left side.
   e. Trade places with your partner.
4. While alone, pretend to go through the motions of making sliding and hook tackles.
   a. Find a soft and safe area to practice.
   b. Try it in slow motion with a partner acting as the dribbler.

8
Defenders, Midfielders, Strikers

You are in the middle of the field with the ball under control at your feet. An opponent in front of you is waiting for a chance to tackle the ball. A teammate on your right is guarded and not free. Another teammate is running toward you but suddenly stops about ten yards away and calls for you to make a quick pass. At the same time, a teammate on your left slips away from a defender and is in the clear for a moment. Still controlling the ball you remain alert to "catch and spot" these play possibilities while your teammates switch their field positions to give you a chance to pass the ball.

Soccer is an exciting game! Because the action is fast most young players want to play only one position. Don't rush! Try playing all the other positions, too. Learn the duties that are assigned to each position. When you have learned about the special qualifications that are needed for the different positions, you will play a smarter game. As you grow bigger and stronger you will be able to choose the position that is best for you.

NAMES OF PLAYERS

The names of the eleven soccer players that make up a team are usually divided into four groups: the defenders, or fullbacks, or backs; the midfielders, or link players; the attackers, or strikers; and the goalkeeper, or goalie.

The number of players assigned to each group will depend on the formation or system of play a team uses. (You will learn about the goalkeeper in Chapter Nine and the systems of play in Chapter Ten.)

QUALIFICATIONS FOR THE DEFENDERS

These players are often known as fullbacks or backs. What kind of players make successful defenders? They must be good at helping the goalkeeper defend the goal and at preventing the opponents from scoring. They must be prepared to make strong tackles and to intercept the opponents' passes. Above all, they must work closely with the other defenders and the goalkeeper in keeping calm when things are not going well.

DUTIES OF THE DEFENDERS

1. Defenders must know the team formations and systems of play.
2. Before each game players should be told whether they are to cover one particular player (player-on-player defense) or a certain area on the field (zone defense).
3. They must know when to pass to their own goalkeeper.
4. During game action they should know when to use the skills of charging, trapping, and obstructing.
5. They must protect and cover the goal when the goalkeeper goes out for the ball.

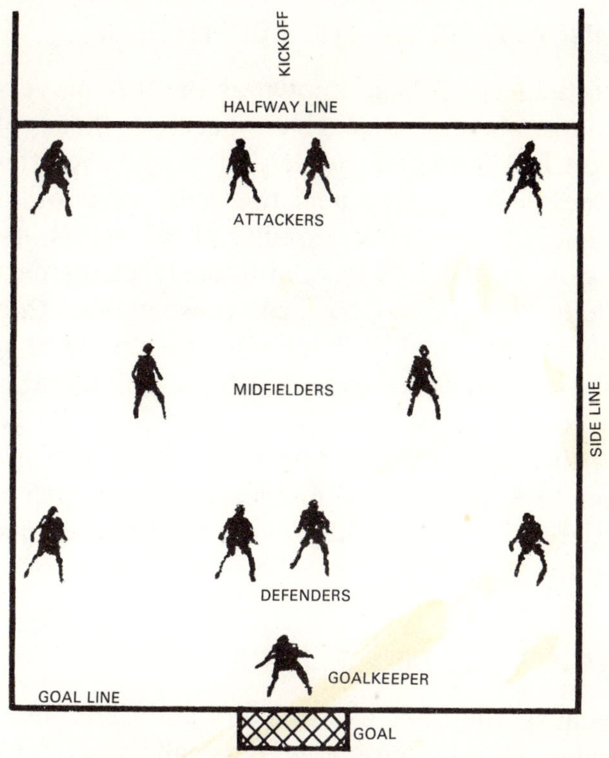

SAMPLE POSITION AND NAMES OF PLAYERS

6. They should know when to make short passes to a teammate or long kicks toward the opponent's goal.
7. They must be careful not to make passes across the field in front of their own goal area.
8. They should know when to *first time* the ball out of the danger zone or control the ball and start the offense.

Quite a list of duties, isn't it? Start practicing now. Learn to tackle, charge, trap, head, dodge, and pass. Play pick-up team soccer, even if you are short the full number of players. Little by little, you will learn the game and soon find yourself ready for team play.

QUALIFICATIONS OF THE MIDFIELDERS

The midfielders are also known as the link players. The name link players was given because these players formed a link between the defenders and the attackers. Midfielders usually play near the *center* or *middle* of the field. They must think rapidly at all times because possession of the ball is continuously changing in the midfield area. Some coaches call these players the "field generals of the attack." Often they are small but aggressive players. They are expected to be quick and nimble and to possess a lot of stamina. They must be good at getting the ball to their team's attackers who are in a position to score. These midfielders must also play a smart defensive game and prevent their opponents from moving the ball.

DUTIES OF THE MIDFIELDERS

1. Because they act as attackers and defenders, midfielders should know how to use all the soccer skills.
2. They must be ready to shift or change positions on the field with the team's attackers or defenders if the style of play calls for this strategy.
3. They must know when to use their feinting, dodging, and ball control skills to fool their opponents.
4. They must know when to make an accurate pass to an attacker in the front line.
5. They must know when to use the skills of dribbling, charging, trapping, heading, and tackling.
6. They must know when to run with the ball to confuse the opponent's defense.

QUALIFICATIONS OF THE ATTACKERS

The attackers are also called *strikers* or *forwards.* They play on the forward line that is nearest to the opponent's goal. These players are often assigned to play in a specified area on the field. The attacking players located nearest the goal are called the *inside strikers.* They must excel at shooting with either foot and also at heading the ball for a score. Attackers assigned closer to the sidelines are known as *outside strikers* or *left* and *right wingers.* Some of these players are stronger right foot shooters and kickers, while others are better at playing with the left foot. The offensive system used by the team will decide to which positions these players are assigned. All attackers should be very skillful at shooting and heading for a goal. They also should be good at trapping, ball control, and at making accurate passes and quick screens.

DUTIES OF THE ATTACKERS

1. They must know when to set up plays that will score.
2. They must know when and how to spread the defense by playing close to the sidelines.
3. They must be ready to make fast tackles when on defense.
4. All attackers should know when to dribble, feint, pivot, or go into a change-of-pace movement.
5. They must know one another's habits and signals, which can help during quick-action play.
6. During a game, each attacker must know when to switch and change positions with another attacker to make the play successful.
7. They must always keep an eye on the location of the other attackers on the field.

The game is filled with action and excitement whether you play the position of a defender, midfielder, or striker. Study and practice the skills required for the different positions. You will see the importance of learning one another's habits in order to develop good team play.

HELPFUL HINTS

Study these hints carefully. They will help you enjoy the game and also become a better team player.

Defenders. Try to stay between your goal and the opponent you are covering.

Defenders. Try not to block the view of your goalkeeper. This means you must know one another's playing habits.

Defenders. Move up the field to support your midfielders only when you are sure that the area closer to the goal is protected.

Midfielders. Always try to advance the ball to one of your strikers (attackers).

Midfielders. Try to recapture the ball when your opponents have possession of it.

Midfielders. Be ready at all times to support your strikers when they have the ball.

Strikers. When you have the ball, always try to set up a situation that will give your team the best scoring play.

Strikers. Be alert to keep the opponent's defenders from setting up plays when they have the ball in the area of the field where you are playing.

Strikers. When receiving a pass from a teammate, you have the responsibility to move in on or meet the ball at the right moment for a good shot at the goal.

The drills you must work on should include those skills that are listed under *qualifications* for the different positions. Once you learn the skills found in the earlier chapters you will be ready to put them to work in your practice game situations. You may practice on some drills alone. If you have one or more friends for your practices, see that you assign each person to a different player's position. Later on you may wish to change positions with your friends so everyone will get the chance to practice in the different positions. Some drills may have all the players practicing on offensive team skills, while other times you may include players on both defense and offense.

9
How to Be a Goalkeeper

There is one player on each team who performs different skills and who wears a different colored uniform than the other soccer players. Fans and coaches call this player the goalkeeper, who is said to be fearless and to move like an acrobat or ballet dancer. Much of the action of the game takes place in front of the *goalie.* When the ball is in the penalty area, the goalkeeper is the only player allowed to touch the ball with the hands.

The goalkeeper is responsible for preventing the ball from going between the goal posts and under the crossbar for a score. This player is the last line of defense. A goalie must not lose control even when being badgered or heckled by opponents. Instead, this player must remain calm and courageous in the face of the most pressing attack. This is why the skills needed by a goalkeeper involve good, sure hands and nimble, springy legs.

DUTIES OF THE GOALKEEPER

1. A goalkeeper must know the team defense and system of play.

2. S/he must know how to work closely with the defenders on his or her team.
3. S/he must give pep talks and directions to teammates during the game action.
4. S/he must know how to catch and control the ball between the chest and knees.
5. S/he must know when to dive and fall to the right, left, or to the front and how to protect the ball with the hands, chest, and knees.
6. S/he must know when to jump for the ball and punch, tip, strike, or deflect the ball over the crossbar or outside of the goal posts.
7. S/he must decide when to throw (pass) the ball or when to kick it.
8. S/he must know how to play the wind, or a wet ball, or a curve ball (banana curve) or other ball actions.
9. S/he must decide when it is best to leave the goal area.
10. S/he must know the different positions to take in the *mouth* (front area) of the goal in order to stop the attackers who are approaching from different angles.

These duties tell a story about the one player who often seems to be standing alone near the goal. However, the players, fans, and coaches know that the goalkeeper must be ready at any moment to move like a ballet dancer, acrobat, high jumper, diver, catcher, thrower, or kicker.

Get started by putting these duties in your notebook. Practice each of the skills one at a time. Before you know it, you will not only be talking like a goalkeeper, but playing like one, too!

GOALKEEPER ACTION PLAYS

Here are some of the more important skills and plays a goalkeeper should learn and practice.

Rights of a Goalkeeper. A goalkeeper staying inside the penalty area is allowed to catch, carry, or strike the ball with the hands or arms. This player may bounce, dribble, or toss the ball in the air and catch it any number of times as long as no more than four steps are taken. Immediately after completing the four steps, the goalkeeper must get rid of the ball within three seconds. This player has the privilege and right to throw, punt, or drop kick the ball any time within the four steps allowed. A goalkeeper cannot be charged by opponents in any way while having possession of the ball. Possession of the ball includes the times when the goalkeeper is in the act of bouncing, dropping the ball for a kick, or tossing the ball upward and catching it.

Goalkeeper Ready Stance. A top goalkeeper is always in a *ready stance* position when an opponent is about to take a shot at the goal. To get into this position, start by placing your feet about shoulder width apart with the knees slightly bent. Lean a bit forward with your weight equally distributed on the front of your feet, toward the toes. Bring your arms forward and out, with the elbows bent slightly. The palms of your hands should be turned outward toward your opponents. You are now in a well-balanced stance ready to shift, shuffle, slide, dive, or spring into action in any direction.

Catching Ground Balls in Front. To *catch ground balls coming directly toward you*, get ready quickly and face the ball. Place your feet close together and hold your legs almost straight. Bend at the waist and drop your arms. Keep your hands close together with your fingers well

1) STRAIGHT FROM FRONT

2) CATCH FROM SIDE

3) AFTER CATCH PROTECTION

GOALKEEPER GROUND BALL CATCHES

spread and a few inches from the ground with the palms facing the approaching ball. At the moment the ball meets your hands, the arms and hands should give and move back a little toward you so you can scoop the ball up without having it bounce away. With the elbows close to your body, quickly bring the ball up and tuck it into the pit of your stomach. Your chest, shoulders, and head should be well over the ball for control.

Catching Ground Balls to the Side. Here is what you do to *catch ground balls coming at you from the side.* Your foot nearest the ball should make a quick step toward the direction of the ball. Get into a comfortable kneeling position with the same foot and leg. Place the heel of your opposite foot close to the leg in a kneeling position. You are ready to *catch* the ball and *control* it in the same way you did for the ball shot directly at you.

FLY BALL STOMACH CATCH

Catching Balls between Knees and Shoulders. You must act speedily to *catch a ball shot between your knees and shoulders.* Start by keeping your eyes on the ball. Then move toward the flying ball. Your feet are about a foot apart with the knees slightly bent and your weight equally distributed forward toward the toes. Stretch your arms forward holding your palms upward in a cupped position ready to catch the ball. Your elbows are bent close to your body. At the moment the ball hits your hands, they should give with the ball as you guide it quickly toward the pit of your stomach. Wrap your hands and arms around the ball. Your chest, shoulders, and head should be well over the ball for control.

Note. Later in the chapter you will discover that after the ball is under control, you must learn how to get rid of it as quickly and accurately as possible.

OVER HEAD CATCH

Balls Caught Overhead. You must have good coordination, timing and explosive power in your legs to *catch balls shot over your head.* Keep your eyes on the ball and move toward the flying ball as quickly as possible. Get ready to *time* your jump for the ball when the ball is about to approach overhead. Make the jump with your arms and hands stretched well above your head. Have your palms facing the ball and keep your hands close together so they form a cup. You must be ready to catch the ball while you are at the highest point of the jump. Make the catch with your hands. At the height of your jump you should also have one of your knees raised slightly. This acts as protection against opponents who may charge into you by mistake. The ball is controlled by hugging it quickly to your chest, with your shoulders and head drawn down over the ball.

Diving to Catch Fly Balls. To catch fly balls by diving for them requires the agility of a ballet dancer and the speed of an end player in the American game of football. It is an action play that is very exciting for the fans. You need explosive leg power and sure hands to catch and control the ball. After the catch you must know how to fall safely. *Because of the possible dangers involved you should not practice diving catches without instructions from your parents, teacher, or coach.*

Diving catches are made by using your legs in a springlike way, which will drive your body toward the ball. Your arms are stretched up, with your palms facing the ball in a cupped position. As the ball hits your hands you should start bringing it in to your chest area. During the catch your legs are stretched back, but your knees should bend quickly toward the ball at the moment of landing. To lighten the force of your fall, try to land on the ball, then on your arm, shoulder, and upper part of

1) MAKING THE SIDE DIVE

2) SOFT LANDING—HOLDING BALL

3) PROTECTING BALL

DIVING HIGH BALL CATCH

your body. Control the ball by bringing it in to your chest and hugging it tightly.

Diving to Catch Ground Balls. Dives to catch ground balls are made in almost the same way as those made for the fly balls. The big difference is that your dive for ground balls is started by letting the thighs, hips, and legs touch the ground first. Your arms are stretched out to catch and control the ball in the same way as you reached for the fly ball. Protect the ball quickly by hugging it to your chest, and then by rolling over it with your shoulders and arms. *Parents or teachers should assist you in learning this dive before you try it in a game situation.*

Punching and Striking the Ball. These are actions taken when you can't reach a ball to catch it or too many opponents are blocking you from making a safe catch. For a shot that is above your head, you must time your jump so you meet the ball at its highest point. The ball is punched, tipped, or deflected over the crossbar with the knuckles of one or both of your clenched fists. If you can't punch the ball over the crossbar, try to punch it as far back into the sideline areas of the playing field as you can. This clears the ball away from the goal area. Balls shot near the inside of the upright goal posts should be punched or tapped *to the outside of the post.* Some goalies like to *strike* at the ball by using the side of their fist instead of their knuckles. Choose the method that works best for you.

Goalkeeper Throwing the Ball. Throwing and passing are additional ways that a goalkeeper has to clear the ball from the goal area. The ball may be thrown to a teammate nearby or far away from the goal. There are

PUNCHING BALL OVER CROSSBAR

two ways a goalie may throw the ball: *underhand* or *overhand* (sidearm).

The Underhand Throw. This throw is the most accurate for getting the ball to a free teammate nearby. When you have possession of the ball, try to look for a teammate who is free of an opponent. Have your throwing hand under and behind the ball, while your other hand rests lightly on top of the ball for control. As you lean forward, start swinging the ball down and back to get

1) LOOKING AT TARGET

2) FOLLOW THROUGH

LOW UNDERHAND THROW

ready for the throw. Take a quick step toward the target with the foot opposite the throwing arm. Keeping your eyes on the receiver make a smooth, swinging underhand motion, releasing the ball along the ground for a perfect roller at the feet of your teammate. Then follow through with your throwing hand pointing at the target. The whole action is similar to that of an underhand softball pitch.

Overhand (or Sidearm) Throw. This throw is best used for reaching a long-distance target (teammate). It is thrown when you have no other choice because there are no teammates close by to roll the ball toward. Hold the ball with both hands, the same way you did for the underhand throw. Raise the ball quickly to your side to about shoulder height. Make a good step forward toward your target and release the ball with plenty of force behind it. The complete action looks like a baseball pitcher making an overhead or sidearm pitch, except the arm is stiffer in the soccer throw.

Punting the Ball. Goalies use the *punt* to send the ball a long distance away from the goal. It is a smart play to use when you can't find a teammate open to receive a rolling or overhead throw. You must remember that you have only four steps to get the punt away.

Hold the ball comfortably with both hands a little under and to the side of the ball. This will help you control the ball. (As you grow older you may wish to use only one hand on the ball.) Hold the ball in front of you about waist high and take a quick, short step forward with your kicking foot. Then take a regular-sized step with your other foot. Your kicking foot is now behind you, ready to make the punt. As your kicking leg begins to move forward, lower the ball and release it just above knee height. Point the toes of your kicking foot forward and a bit inward, keeping your ankle rigid. All your weight should be on the other foot. Now comes the kick! With a nice whipping action, your kicking foot meets the ball with the instep at about knee height. After the punt, straighten your knee and continue the kicking action for a good follow-through. The action is almost the same as the one you use for the instep volley kick.

HELPFUL HINTS

A goalkeeper must give confidence to all teammates throughout the game.

S/he must always work closely with the team's defenders.

GOALKEEPER PUNT

1) READY STEP—ARMS FORWARD

2) THE KICK

3) FOLLOW-THROUGH

S/he must know how to play on a rainy or windy day and in cold weather.
S/he must be ready to stop a ball from bouncing over his or her head. S/he always moves forward to get it or stays back and waits for the ball until after the bounce. S/he quickly decides which action to use!
S/he must make an effort to direct every ball toward the sidelines and away from the goal area and center portion of the field.
S/he must fall on the ball only when there is no other way to stop or control it.
S/he must always strike or punch the ball when surrounded by opponents.
After the ball is caught, s/he must throw a pass to an open teammate as quickly as possible so the team can start on an offensive attack.

GOALKEEPER DRILLS

1. *Goalkeeper Ready Stance.* Get in front of a mirror in your room and start practicing shifting and shuffling in different directions. Mark a goal line a few feet from the wall. Stand about a yard in front of the line. Repeat these moves outdoors and add the sliding, jumping, and diving movements from the ready stance positions.

2. *Catching the Ball.* Find a wall clear of windows; a soccer goal net; a baseball batter's backstop or cage; or a fenced-in tennis area.
   a. *Without the ball* pretend you are going for the different catches (rolling, knee height, overhead, side, and diving).

b. Toss a ball against a backstop or solid wall and make the different catches.

c. Have a partner standing several feet away toss the ball toward you so you can try the different catches. From a distance of twelve yards away have a partner *kick* the ball softly toward you to practice the same catches. Change positions with your partner so each of you get a chance to practice goalkeeping.

d. Have your partner increase the distance and speed of the tosses and kicks as you improve.

e. Have a partner stand with the ball about 25 yards away from you. First your partner should dribble and try to get past you for a goal. Later your partner should try dribbling and then take a *shot* at the goal from a distance *behind* a ten-yard marker. Have your partner approach the goal from different angles.

f. Try this drill with two or more players attempting to score at the same time.

g. *A rapid fire drill.* This drill will give you a workout and fun at the same time. You must have about ten soccer balls placed on the ground about 12 to 15 yards from the goal. Get into position in front of the goal. On the word "go" ask a partner to kick one ball at a time as rapidly as possible toward the goal. How many goals can you stop? See that each person gets the opportunity to practice goalkeeping.

3. *Punching and Striking the Ball.* Use the same kind of practice area as in the other drills.

a. Pretend you are punching or striking the ball over the crossbar or outside the goal posts.

b. Have a partner toss a ball just below the height

of the crossbar and try punching or striking the ball *over the crossbar.* Have the ball tossed close to the inside of one of the upright goalposts and try to tip, tap, or punch it outside of the post.

c. Increase the distance and speed of the toss as you improve your movements. Let each partner have a chance at goalkeeping.

4. *Throwing the Ball.* Practice the different throws alone by throwing the ball toward a bare wall or open area. Make up your own drills with a partner.

5. *Punting the Ball.* Locate a clear, open field and practice the punting play with a partner.

10
Systems of Play and Game Strategy

Players, coaches and fans constantly read and hear about the *systems of play* that a team uses during a game. They watch the teams line up on the field for the kickoff. The way the teams line up is called a *formation.*

Different formations are used for offensive or defensive strategy. Each player is given a specific assignment. On offense, more players are assigned to dribble, pass, head, and shoot the ball trying to score. On defense, more players block, tackle, and intercept passes, trying to prevent a score. There are many systems, and a wise coach will choose the right one for his or her team.

WHAT DECIDES A SYSTEM OF PLAY?

The best soccer teams in the world are often known and recognized by the system of play they use. The players practice and play together for many years. Some coaches today try to combine the best from many teams' systems.

Systems or styles of play do not always win games. *It's the players' experience and special skills that decide the formation and system a coach selects for a game.* They consider the opponent's strengths and weaknesses when picking a system to play. Using a certain system helps you know what your duties are and which responsibilities belong to your teammates.

For example, choosing a formation is often decided by how well the midfielders can:

1. Support their attackers.
2. Cover for their defensive players.
3. Cover both the width and length of the field.

A system is only a *pattern to arrange* play in an orderly way. In soccer no matter what system is used, the players remain free to make their own on-the-spot game decisions during important situations or when helping teammates.

BALL MOVEMENT AND PLAYER POSITION

Your movements in a soccer game are determined mainly by the movement and location of the ball during a fast-action game. This action often calls for players to change the plays and formations that were diagrammed or drawn on paper before the game. While the action around the ball is going on, the fans usually miss the constant movements that are made by the players who are not near the ball. These players are shifting, sprinting, or switching into different field positions in order to be ready to make an offensive or defensive play.

THE BEST SYSTEM OF PLAY

Don't spend a lot of time now worrying about fancy formations and plays. *Your time should be spent on having fun* while practicing and learning the soccer skills and duties of the different positions.

A team of young players should use a simple system that gives it a chance to improve in the greatest number of skills. Later, these practiced skills will make the team ready to handle the many different play situations that are selected by the coach.

TEAM FORMATIONS

The different systems of play suggest the kind of strategy a team might use in a game. Are the players in position for a *rough defensive formation*? A *strong offensive formation*? Or a *balanced team formation*? This is the guessing game that goes on among the players and coaches. It is called good strategy and tactics. Each team decides well before the game on how best to outplay and outsmart the other team.

Let's take a look at some of the team formations (systems) that are popular with both beginners and more experienced teams.

Note. Soccer formations are explained and drawn on paper by starting near your own goal and working forward toward the opponent's goal. The goalkeeper is not often shown in the diagram because everyone knows that the position of this player seldom changes.

The W-M Formation. This is one of the most popular formations used by beginning players. It is a formation that gives your team equal coverage for defensive and offensive play.

The "M" is formed by the five players who are positioned nearest to your goal. The three players closest to your goal are defenders. The two players forming the top parts of the "M" act as both midfielders or defenders.

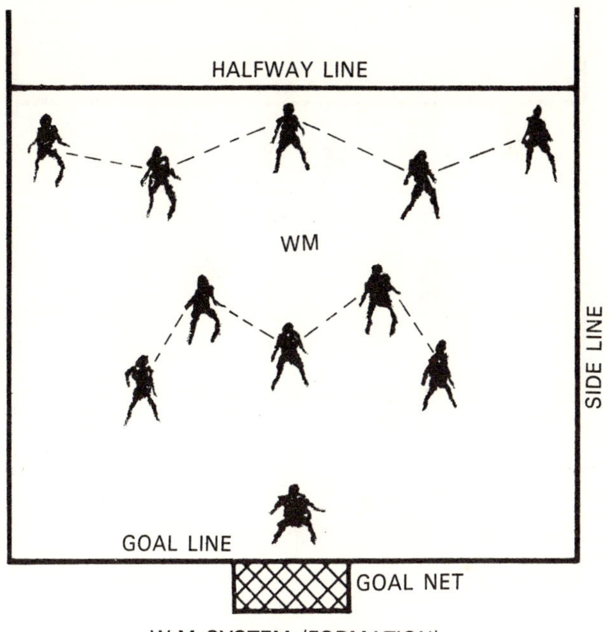

W-M SYSTEM (FORMATION)

The "W" is formed by teammates who are farther up toward the center of the field. The three players nearest to the opponent's goal are the attackers. The two players forming the bottom part of the "W" are ready to play as attackers or midfielders. The goalkeeper is in position in front of the goal.

During the game your teammates are constantly trying to get into the field position that is required by the formation your team is using.

The 4-2-4 Formation. This is used by many of the best teams in the world. This system is often called a *balanced formation* because it gives your team equal coverage of the field on both defense and offense. The back four players closest to the goal are defenders. The front

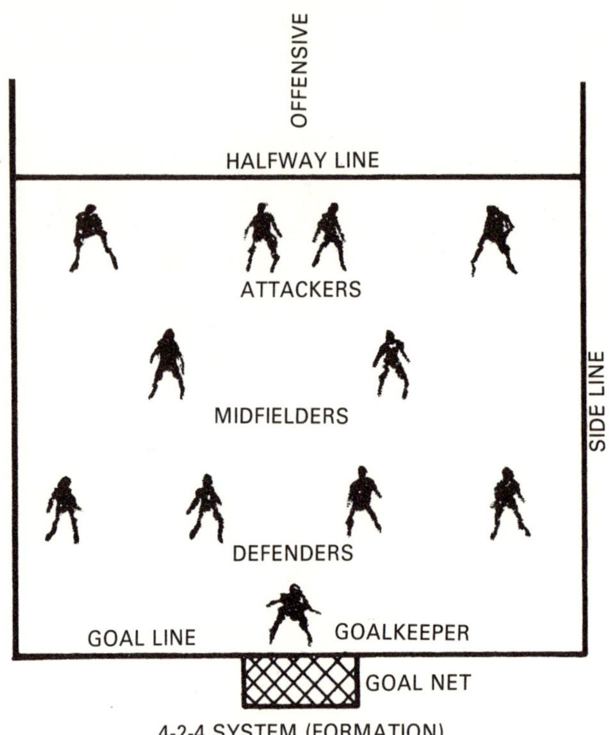

4-2-4 SYSTEM (FORMATION)

middle have the job of link players or midfielders. When the attackers need help the link players can change the formation to make five or six players on offense. If the defenders need help the two midfielders can make it five or six players on defense. This system of play demands a lot of work from the two link players.

The 4-3-3 Formation. This system of play is used by some of the best teams in the world. It allows a team to use a formation that is *strong on defense.* You have four players spread out as defenders, three players on duty as midfielders, and three are ready as strikers, or attackers. The goalkeeper is guarding the goal.

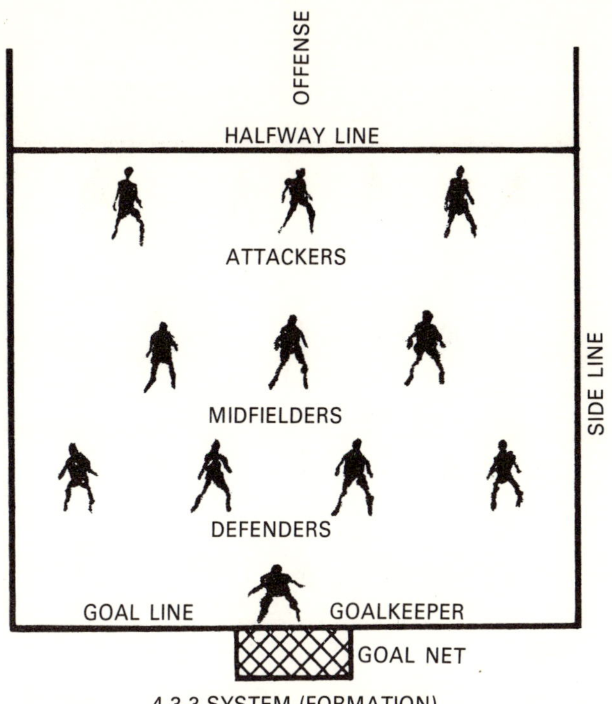

4-3-3 SYSTEM (FORMATION)

The 3-3-4 Formation. This is another system that is widely used by top teams. This formation is chosen when a team wants *strength on offense.* You have three defenders, three midfielders, and four attackers.

More Formations. Other formations are given names like 2-3-5, "V" or Arrowhead, Spearhead or Wedge, Unbalanced, and Inside Floating. After the end of each play, you and your teammates quickly move into the team's favorite formation before the next play starts.

Start your practice on the most simple systems first and don't spend a lot of time on the more advanced formations. Your teacher or coach will decide which system is best for your team.

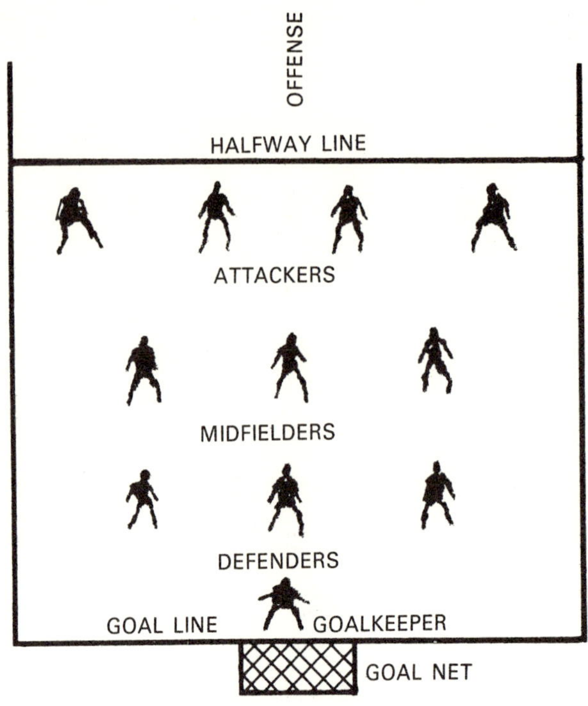

3-3-4 SYSTEM (FORMATION)

MORE STRATEGY

Soccer has many exciting plays just like other team sports. It's very satisfying to the players and fans when they see a good play work. It shows that the players and coaches have practiced extra-long hours to develop special moves that can outsmart the other team. Everyone knows that a good play shows good *team strategy.*

These plays are usually set up or planned on paper before a game. Each player is told ahead of time how to handle the special play situations.

Here are additional situations that you and your teammates may wish to work up for some plays. Ask your coach, teacher, or an older person who knows the game to give you extra help if you need it.

1. Plays that are used on offense and defense when a *direct free kick* is about to be made.
2. *Kick-off* plays that are used on offense and defense.
3. Plays that are used on offense and defense for an *indirect free kick.*
4. Offensive and defensive *corner-kick* plays.
5. Offensive and defensive *throw-in* plays.
6. Plays used on offense and defense for an *offside trap.*

It certainly seems like a lot of responsibility and work! Actually you will catch on to these special play skills quicker than you think. Because you have already learned the earlier skills, you will experience a steady improvement as you *continue to practice* and grow smarter and stronger. Coaches will know when you and your teammates are ready to try the more advanced plays.

Start going to soccer games. Watch the teams on TV. Read all about the game in newspapers and magazines. Can you spot the kind of systems and special plays both teams are using.

Put the best formations and special plays you see in your *Soccer Notebook.* List them under "Special Plays." Work on new formations and plays by yourself and with your friends. It's fun trying them out in practice!

11
Equipment

It's fun to play soccer. You can play on a playground or in an open field, vacant lot, sandy beach, or indoor gym. All you need is a round ball and a pair of sneakers. Wear your old clothes.

Big-league players require more equipment because they play in championship tournaments. This equipment is needed to play fast-action soccer, so that neither team has an advantage during a game. The articles of clothing that the players wear are called personal equipment. The supplies on the soccer field are known as field equipment.

PERSONAL EQUIPMENT

Uniforms often belong to the school, university, or soccer club. The uniforms consist of jerseys (shirt or blouse), shorts, shoes, stockings, and shin guards.

Jerseys (Shirt or Blouse). Each player has two jerseys. A light-colored jersey is worn when the team plays on the home field. The dark uniform is worn only when the team plays away from home. In this way two teams playing against each other never wear jerseys of the same color.

Shorts. The same pair of shorts can be worn for games at home and away. The shorts come in different colors to match the jerseys. They are made just like boxer shorts and can be washed easily.

Shoes. Players wear different types of soccer shoes. Usually they are made of very strong leather uppers with rubber or plastic soles. Most of them are low-cut and have molded cleats made of plastic, nylon, or rubber.

Stockings (Socks). A pair of sweat socks is worn under the long stockings that reach just below the knees.

Protective Shinguards. Players wear lightweight plastic shinguards under their stockings. These guards protect the shins if a player is kicked by mistake.

Soccer Balls. The finest soccer balls are made of leather, while others are made of rubber. The two most popular leather balls are known as the 32-panel and the 18-panel. Each of the 32 separate pieces of leather are hand-sewn or stitched together. Each piece is in the shape of a *pentagon,* or five sided. The 18-panel ball has 18 larger pieces of leather. Each panel is shaped like a rectangle and has four sides.

Official leather balls must not be more than 28 inches or less than 27 inches round. At the beginning of the game the ball must not weigh more than 16 ounces (454.4 grams) and not less than 14 ounces (397.6 grams). There

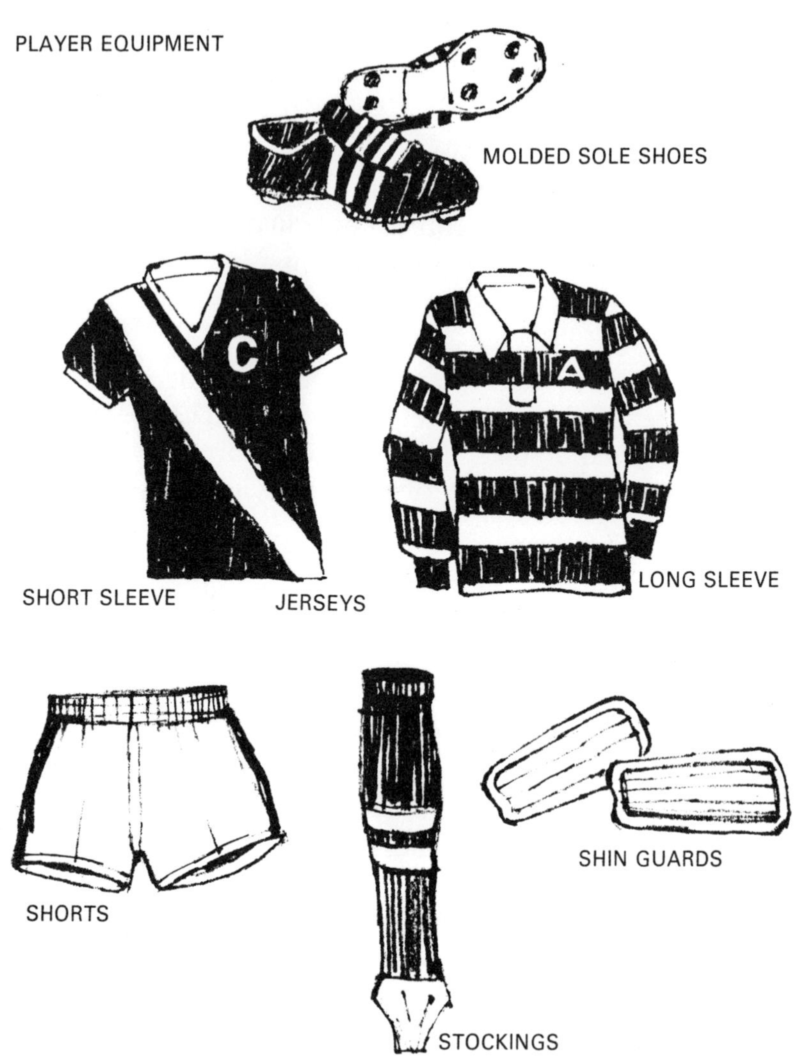

are official *junior-sized balls* that are used for games in the younger soccer leagues.

Goalie Equipment. The goalkeepers wear extra protective equipment. They have specially designed sweaters, jerseys, and shorts with quilted padding to give them

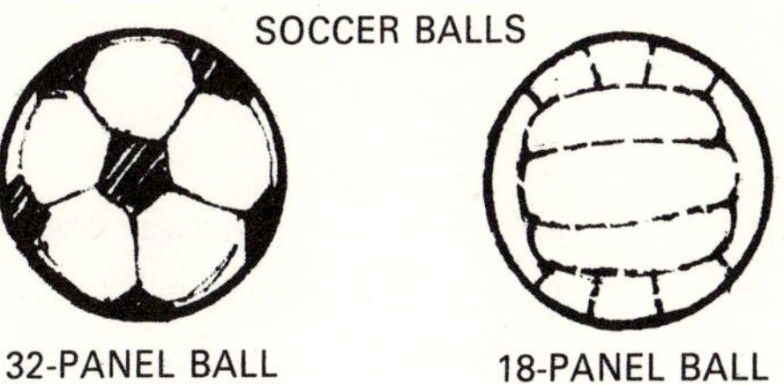

32-PANEL BALL 18-PANEL BALL

extra protection. They may wear *knee* and *elbow pads* and an extra-long *body vest* that has padding in the chest and hip areas. Special gloves are worn when the weather is cold or damp.

OTHER PERSONAL EQUIPMENT

Warm-up Suit. This consists of a jacket and long pants, which are worn over a player's uniform. It is used before

SPECIAL GOALKEEPER UNIFORM

game time and when a player is practicing and loosening up.

Parka and Hood. This is a one-piece garment that is worn like a coat. It is worn over the uniform to keep a player warm and dry when the weather is cold or when it is raining.

Eyeglass Protector. It is worn over a player's regular glasses for extra protection. But only certain kinds can be used in games.

Note. Any equipment that may be dangerous should not be used in a game, i.e. shoes with nails, eyeglass protectors with metal or wire frames.

OFFICIALS' EQUIPMENT

At ordinary games one or two officials are enough. But for important games as many as ten officials may take charge. If *boys* and *girls* use the National Federation of State High School Associations (NFSHSA) rules, the officials are two referees, two lines people, two timers, two scorekeepers, and two ball persons. For *girls* using the National Association for Girls and Women in Sports (NAGWS) rules, the officials are two umpires, two timekeepers, two scorekeepers, and four lines people.

For the boys' games, referees and lines people wear black and white shirts, black shorts, black stockings, and soccer shoes. For the girls' games umpires and lines people wear black and white blouses or shirts, black or navy shorts, slacks, or skirts, and soccer shoes.

The Referees and Umpires. Referees are the officials for the boys' games listed by the National Federation of State High School Associations. Umpires are the officials for the girls' games only, listed by the National

Association for Girls and Women in Sports (NAGWS). These officials have full control of the game. One of the two referees or umpires is chosen as the final official for a game. Both referees wear whistles around their necks. They use the whistle to begin the game with a kickoff, and for penalty kicks, drop balls, out-of-play balls, fouls, and to signal that a goal has been scored. They also carry a rule book with which to settle arguments, if necessary.

Each referee or umpire covers the action that takes place on his or her half of the field.

Lines People and Ball Persons. Lines people help the referee or umpire decide at what point the ball crossed the sideline. The *ball persons* for the boys and the *lines people* for the girls have one extra game ball ready on each side of the field. They quickly deliver one to the official or a player when it is requested. The boys' ball persons and the girls' lines people also have the duty to chase and retrieve the balls that travel outside the playing area. This prevents delay of the game.

Scorekeepers. One scorekeeper from each team is selected to record the action of the game. One is chosen as the official scorekeeper. Both scorekeepers are supplied with scoresheets, pads of paper, pencils, and a horn. Scorekeepers have a list of all the players and substitutes for each team. They record how each goal was made and what team won the game. The action and play of each player and team is also recorded. The scorekeepers are located at the officials' table near the half-way line, five yards from the sideline. The name of the final official is also noted on the scoresheet. Substitutes must report to the officials' table to have their names put on the scoresheet. The scorekeeper must sound the horn to let the umpire or referee know that a new player wants to enter the game.

Timekeepers. There are two timekeepers, one from each team. But one acts as the official timekeeper. Both timekeepers are ready with a stopwatch or stopclock, horn, siren, or pistol. They keep a record of the playing time. They must know when to stop the clock for a goal, for the award of a penalty kick, or other out-of-bounds plays that delay the game. The clock or watch is started every time the ball is put back into play. The timekeepers cooperate very closely with the referee or umpire. They are also seated at the officials' table off the field near the half-way line.

FIELD EQUIPMENT

A soccer field is shaped like a rectangle. It is marked with white lines. The size of the field changes with the age of the players and the league they represent. A crossbar and goal posts are located at each end of the field.

The center of the field is marked by a *half-way line.* Girls' fields may also have a *restraining line* drawn five yards along each side of the half-way line. Boys' fields have a sixty-foot circle marked exactly in the center of the field. Markings for the girls' penalty area are shaped like a half-circle, while those for the boys' area are shaped like a rectangle.

Goal Posts. The goal posts are 24 feet apart and stand eight feet high. Eight feet above the ground a crossbar is fastened to both posts. The crossbars and posts are made of wood, aluminum, or steel pipe.

Goal Nets. A goal net is fastened to the goal posts and extends the length of the crossbar. The net is stretched back and set into the ground behind the crossbar and goal posts. Nets are made out of regular twine, nylon, or wire mesh screen.

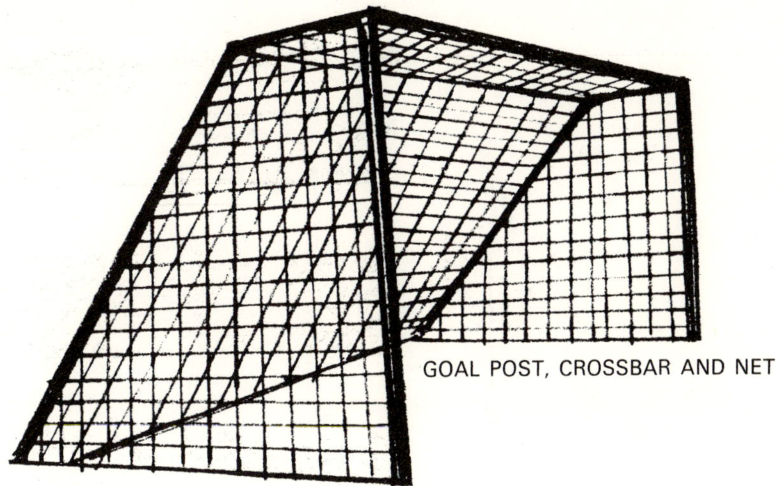

GOAL POST, CROSSBAR AND NET

Corner Flags. A pole with a flag is set into the ground at each corner of the field. The pole must be at least five feet high. The flag at the top of the pole is about two feet long and one foot wide. Some teams also have a flag post just outside the sideline at each end of the half-way line. Corner posts are made of metal or wood. Some flags are attached to a metal coil spring, which bends easily when a player runs into it. The type of *poles that bend should be used by younger players because they are safer.* The flag may not be removed when a corner kick is awarded.

Team Benches. Team benches are located on each side of the officials' tables, at least ten yards from the sideline. All substitute players must remain in their own team's bench area when they are not playing.

Coaching Area. The coaches must always remain in the players' bench area. They are not allowed to go onto the playing field unless the referee or umpire calls them onto the field.

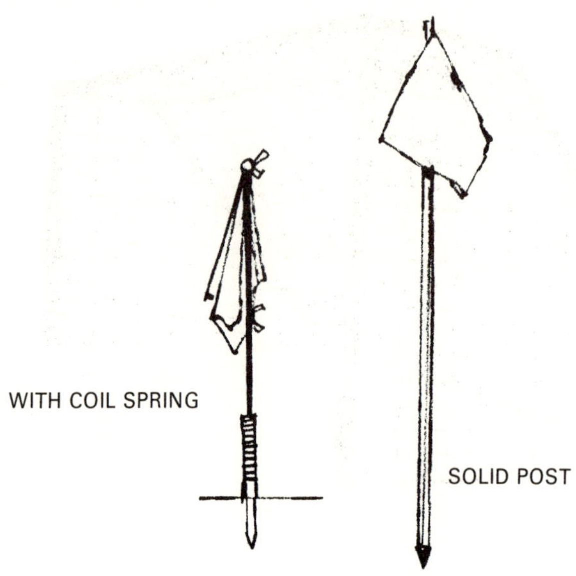

POST AND CORNER FLAGS

Announcer. The announcer's voice is heard over several of the loudspeakers that are located in different sections of the playing area. Before the game, the announcer gives the fans the starting line-up for each team. The fans hear about the new players who enter the game. They are told when a team is penalized and which foul was committed by whom and which player made an outstanding play. The announcer must be very accurate when giving information over the loudspeaker.

You have now seen the personal and field equipment used by big-league players. Behind the scenes, unnoticed, are the field workers who keep the playing area beautifully trimmed and neat. There are trainers who help the players stay in shape. There are doctors who take care of the players when they are sick or have been injured.

Most professional and college players need all this

equipment and assistance. But when these players were young boys and girls, they played a very simple game. They did not have uniforms. They played with only a ball, old shoes, and play clothes. However, by practicing and obeying training rules, they became good team players.

You, too, can become a top player. But you must start at the beginning and learn the game as the big-leaguers did.

12 Getting Ready for the Big Game

The big day is here! Your team is ready to play against another team. But do you know all of the things that must be attended to before you can really play soccer?

Is the competition open to anyone? Are only members of a club allowed to play? Where is the game going to be held? Are you going to use boys' or girls' rules? Or, are you going to use some of the rules from both the boys' and the girls' games? Are you going to have teams made up of both boys and girls? Do you have the right equipment? Is there a competent referee or umpire? What about a scorekeeper, timer, ballpersons and lines people? Do you have a captain?

These and many more questions must be answered before the soccer game starts. Of course, it is most important that each boy and girl be physically fit and trained before the day of the game.

KEEPING FIT

Remember, always keep yourself healthy and strong. Here are some suggestions:

1. Follow the training rules, hints, and exercises in each chapter.
2. Practice as often as you can in a safe place.
3. Report any soreness or bruise to your parents, guardian, coach, teacher, or doctor. A delay in reporting an injury could be serious.
4. Practice good eating habits at home and in school.
5. Get plenty of rest and sleep.
6. Do not neglect your study habits.
7. Keep your body clean.
8. Do not be discouraged if you do not do well at first. *The important thing is that you are healthy in an active sport.*

CHOOSING A FIELD

Where are you going to play? Is it going to be an indoor or an outdoor game?

You must remember that indoor soccer games require a school, club, or park gymnasium. Outdoor soccer usually requires a football, soccer, or baseball field, or another large area. Most regulation indoor and outdoor soccer areas are not available for younger competitors. Do not let the lack of facilities and equipment stop you from competing. But be sure to find a safe place. If you can use an official field or large gymnasium, fine; if not, look for an open space in a park, playground, or large, empty area. Ask the owners of the empty area if you can use it for an outdoor soccer game. Ask your teachers and coaches if the school gymnasium can be used for an indoor game.

Now, pretend that you have your place to play. Let's find out how to make an outdoor soccer field. These instructions can also be used, with very few changes, for indoor soccer competition.

HOW TO MAKE YOUR OWN FIELD

Remove any tin cans, stones, glass, and high weeds. Roll big rocks away from the area so they will not harm anyone. Place all trash in a box and carry it away, or dig a deep hole and bury it. Make the ground as level as possible. Then mark the field.

Marking the Field. The playing lines should be marked with safe material made of white chalk powder. Hardware and sporting goods stores sell such marking material. Another way to mark the field is to use cloth or cardboard. Put a piece of white cloth or cardboard at each corner of the field and at places where the goal, half-way, and girls' restraining lines connect with the sidelines. A bundle of old newspapers or magazines is very good for marking these same spots. Decide if you plan to use the National Federation of State High School Associations (NFSHSA) or the National Association for Girls and Women in Sports (NAGWS) rules. Mark the following lines:

NFSHSA (boys and girls)	*NAGWS (girls)*
1. Goal lines	1. Goal lines
2. Penalty area lines	2. Penalty area lines
3. Goal area lines	3. Restraining lines
4. Center circle	4. Sidelines
5. Sidelines	5. Corner kick marks
6. Corner kick area	6. Half-way lines
7. Half-way lines	7. Goalpost markers
8. Goal post markers	8. Penalty kick mark
9. Penalty kick mark	

Note: Check the illustrations of the two different field markings on pages 144–145 in this chapter.

MEASUREMENTS FOR A JUNIOR SOCCER FIELD

There is no official rule that gives the size of a junior soccer field, but here are several suggestions that are often followed by young teams and elementary schools.

1. Elementary school boys' and girls' fields can measure anywhere from 60 to 100 yards long and 40 to 50 yards wide.
2. Boys' junior high school fields can measure about 100 to 120 yards long and 55 to 75 yards wide. (Also approved for girls by the NFSHSA.)
3. Girls' junior high school fields can measure from 80 to 100 yards long and 40 to 60 yards wide. (Approved by NAGWS.)

PLAYERS' BENCHES

There are two players' benches, one for each team. One is located on each side of the officials' table. They can be made of scrap lumber. Teams may use folding chairs instead of the benches. The coaches also use the team benches.

YOUNG PLAYERS' PERSONAL EQUIPMENT

Never allow a lack of equipment to keep you from playing. Your regular physical education uniforms—gym or boxer-type shorts and T-shirts or blouses—are fine for soccer competition. A pair of sneakers and sweat socks will complete the uniform you need to enjoy soccer.

If you do not have gym uniforms, an old pair of dungarees and a shirt or sweater will do.

Soccer balls are made of leather or rubber. A junior-sized soccer ball is best for the younger player.

Do not plan to purchase regular cleated soccer shoes

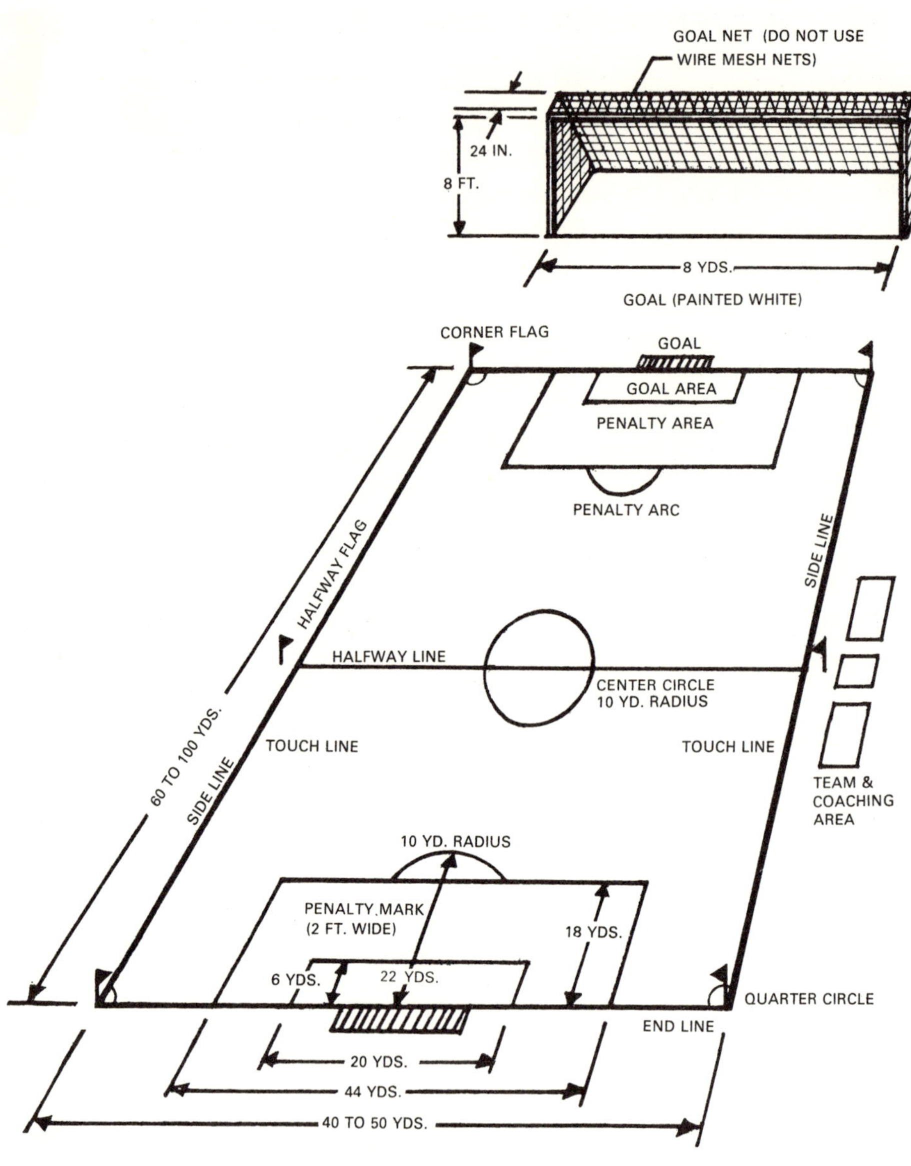

BOYS' JUNIOR SOCCER FIELD

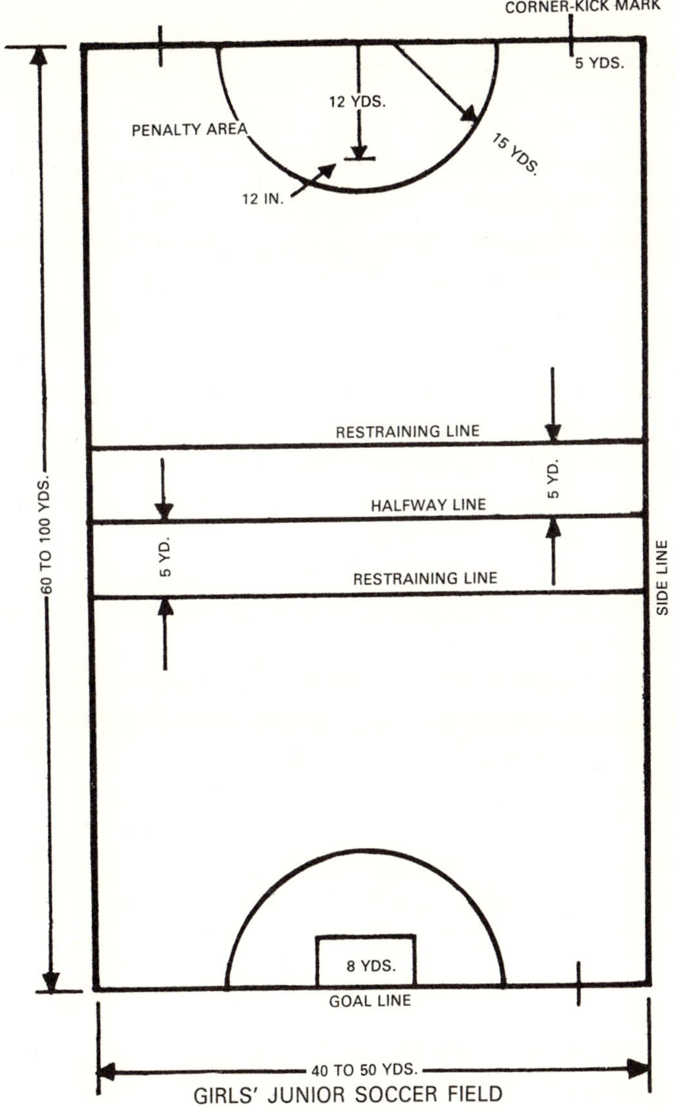

GIRLS' JUNIOR SOCCER FIELD

or shin pads without the advice of your teacher, coach, parents, or guardian.

HOW TO GET UNIFORMS AND EQUIPMENT

Of course, it's nice to play in a full uniform and have all the equipment. But equipment is expensive and many young boys and girls cannot afford to buy everything.

Players can earn money by working together as a team or each player can work for him or herself.

Working as a Team. Let your parents, guardian, or teachers know that your soccer team is going to form work groups to earn money for uniforms and equipment. Keep your eyes open for opportunities to help others, and at the same time help yourselves. Here are some money-making suggestions:

1. Help your neighborhood with a clean-up drive. Clean yards, mend and paint broken fences, cut grass, and water lawns.
2. Collect papers and magazines and sell them.
3. Organize a delivery service for supermarkets, drugstores, or other stores in the community.
4. Give a play, puppet show, or magic show.

Working Alone. There are many fine jobs you can do alone to earn money. It all depends on where you live. Do you live in the city or the country? You can shine shoes, make toys, birdhouses, fish flies, and ash trays.

Learn to make attractive and useful things at school, in your neighborhood park, youth center, church, or settlement house. Join a class in arts and crafts and sell what you make.

Boys and girls who live in the country can earn money by pulling weeds or picking berries and vegetables and crating them. You can gather and candle eggs, tend and

IN UNIFORM AND IN ACTION

feed the farm animals, herd sheep or cattle, clean barns, or dig worms for fishing.

Neighborhood business people oftentimes are interested in helping a youngsters' sports club get started.

Give help where it is needed. But don't try to do anything that is too hard or that will make you neglect your studies. Young athletes get a real thrill when they know they have earned their own uniforms and equipment.

Competing without Uniforms and Equipment. Do not let the lack of a field or regulation uniforms or equipment stop you from taking part in soccer.

Many of our greatest players got their starts when they were young without the best uniforms and equipment. If they didn't have a regular soccer ball, they made one out

IN UNIFORM—READY FOR GAME!

of cloth. They sometimes used a beach ball or a plastic or rubber ball instead of a real soccer ball.

GAME OFFICIALS

Captain. Each team selects a captain. This player should be liked and respected by all of the members of the team. If an argument comes up, the captain represents the team. He settles disputes with the referee or umpire or with the captain of the opposing team.

Coach. In an important game, an older person should act as coach. This person makes all the substitutions and decides who will play the various team positions. The coach sees that the team plays the game according to the rules. If there is no coach, the captain takes care of these duties.

Scorekeeper. Each team has its own scorekeeper. All scoresheets should be saved because they are the only records of the team's work. The scoresheet for each team shows the names of players and their positions, the players making a score, and the number of saves by the goalie.

If a team wants a more complete record, the players should refer to *Chapter Thirteen*, "Scores and Records," for additional information.

Referee, Umpire, Timer. A grownup should act as referee or umpire for an important game. This person should know soccer. It could be your teacher, a parent, an older student, or a member of some local soccer club.

This official must be fair in making decisions. But sometimes game officials do make mistakes. When this happens there is nothing you can do. The referee's or umpire's word is final. The referee or umpire often serves as the timekeeper. But it's best that you try to find another person for this duty.

Ball Persons or Lines People. Use students for these assignments. They must work closely with the referee or umpire.

ARRANGING FOR A GAME

Making arrangements for a game is a big job. Many details must be attended to well ahead of time. The coach, captain, boy, or girl selected as team secretary may make the arrangements in any of several ways:

1. Phone the captain or coach of the other team asking to play against them.
2. Write a letter asking for a game.

3. Visit the other captain or coach and plan the details of the game.

Make sure that the other team is a fair match for yours. Teams should be matched as to grade in school, size, weight, playing ability, and experience. If you play a team that is heavier and bigger than yours, the game will probably be one-sided. It's possible that some of your smaller and younger players may get hurt. Also, you must decide how many girls or boys will be on the field of play at one time.

The captain, coach, or secretary should keep a written record of the games to be played. This record should show:

1. Where the games will be played.
2. The number of players on each team.
3. The exact rules that will be followed (boys', girls', or some of each).
4. The length of the game.
5. The officials for the game.
6. The equipment owned by each team.

After all the arrangements are made, give your teammates as much information as possible about the games they will play.

Choosing for the Kickoff. Whether there is a full team or just a few players on each side, the captains must decide which team shall have the choice of kickoff. This choice is made by the toss of a coin or by guessing.

As the referee or umpire tosses a coin into the air, one of the captains calls for "heads" or "tails." The winner of the toss may choose to kick off or decide which goal to defend during the first period; the loser gets the remaining choice.

Another way to choose is for someone to pick up a handful of pebbles or blades of grass from the ground.

Each captain tries to guess the number of pebbles or blades of grass. The closest guess wins the first choice.

THE INDOOR SOCCER GAME

If the game is planned for indoors, check with your teachers about safety. Windows and exposed lights should be covered with wire mesh screens. Walls should be covered with padded material.

Floor Dimensions. The length and width of the indoor field will be decided by the size of the gymnasium or hall you plan to use.

Most big-league indoor games have no sidelines or goal lines. These games are played on an ice-hockey-sized field. The walls surrounding the field take the place of the boundary lines.

This game allows for more action and scoring. The other dimensions that are different from the outdoor game are:

1. The goals should be 12 feet long and 4 feet high.
2. A 25-foot radius in the shape of a half-circle is marked to show the *goal area.*
3. The penalty spot is marked 20 feet from the center of the goal.
4. The center of the playing field is marked by a spot.

Indoor Game Rules. Some rule changes that are different from the outdoor game are:

1. No more than seven players on a team are allowed to be on the floor at one time.
2. A junior-sized ball with a little air let out (slightly deflated) should be used. This helps to make the ball softer so it can be safely used in a smaller space. A slightly deflated volleyball is also very good.

3. Regular sneakers are used instead of shoes with cleats.
4. No player, not even the goalkeeper, is allowed to use the hands or arms to block shots at the goal. However, you may permit the use of the hands if it is agreed by both teams.
5. There are no throw-ins as in the outdoor game. Balls that go out-of-bounds over the sidelines or wall are passed onto the floor with the side of the foot or a kick-in type of play.
6. There is no offside rule as in the outdoor game.
7. When a ball is tied up against a wall or in a corner by two opposing players, it is put back into play by a dropped ball five yards from the spot where the "trap" occurred. The referee or umpire drops the ball between the two players who originally tied it up.
8. A ball remains in play when it hits the wall and bounces back onto the field of play.
9. The number of substitute players on a team can be decided by the captains or coaches. Free substitution as in ice hockey is allowed. However, the substitute must get the attention of the referee or umpire, or wait until the ball leaves the playing area before going into the game.
10. Teams agree on the length of the game.

It's quite a job getting ready for a big game, isn't it? Probably you had no idea that so many things had to be taken care of. Now you have an idea of what goes on behind the scenes in a big-league soccer club: letters, telegrams, contracts, meetings, and many, many worries. Right now your worries are on a much smaller scale. The important thing to remember is that you are playing soccer because it's fun and you enjoy the game.

MOTHERS ENJOYING SMALL-SPACE SOCCER

EVERYONE PLAYS

Because soccer is truly a *universal game*, you should be ready to play at all times. Boys and girls, men and women, and families everywhere can be seen playing different forms of soccer. Different size balls made out of different materials are used. Rules can be changed for safe play and to meet your situation. Now, go play a game of soccer!

13
Scores and Records

You and your friends get a report card from school that tells you how well you are doing. Did you know that soccer players also receive report cards? Their report cards may look different from the one you get at school, but the cards serve a purpose very much like yours. They show how well the players do their work. How is a soccer player's report card made out? Who prepares the cards? Who figures the player's marks and rates the team's performance?

The record really begins when you start to study and practice for a game. It continues on the soccer field with the work of the referee or umpire. Every time you score or commit a foul it becomes part of your record. Not many fans see the tremendous amount of material that is collected by officials who help to prepare the final report.

OFFICIAL SCOREKEEPER

There is an official scorekeeper for all important games. This official is often hired by the commissioner of a league or school organization, with the agreement of each participating team. The scorekeeper knows the soccer rules and understands the skills of the players.

Upon large sheets of paper s/he fills in and answers many questions about each team and its players. Some of these questions are answered on the *official game program*, which shows the players' names, positions, ages, weights, heights, towns, schools, and past records. But most important, the scorekeeper must have ready a *master game scoring record sheet.*

In different areas around the field and stands, there are reporters from college, school, and community newspapers, as well as radio and TV announcers. They also follow the game closely and keep their own scores and records.

TEAM RECORDS

These are some of the more important team matters the scorekeepers will report on during the game:

1. Name, number, and position of each player in each starting lineup.
2. Name of substitutes entering the game.
3. Number of goal shots tried during the game.
4. Name of team scoring the points and how the score was made.
5. Number of corner kicks in the game.
6. Number of fouls made during the game and officials' warning of players.
7. Number of saves made by the goalkeeper.
8. Outstanding plays and the highlights of the game.

PLAYER RECORDS

These are some of the more important bits of information the scorekeeper records for each player:

1. Number of points made by each player.
2. Number of minutes played by each player.

3. Number of times a player assisted a teammate in making a score.
4. Number of fouls each player committed.
5. Number of shots on goal by each player.

GOALIE RECORDS

Each goalkeeper is graded upon his performance. Taken into account are:

1. Number of saves made in the game.
2. Number of minutes played.
3. How successful the goalie was in making throws, punts, or kicks to a teammate.
4. Strong and weak points of the goalkeeper's game.
5. Goalkeeper's cooperation with other teammates.
6. Number of goals scored on the goalkeeper.
7. Did the goalkeeper have a shutout game?

TEAM SCOREKEEPER

Each team also has a scorekeeper of its own. These club scorekeepers keep an even more detailed record of the players. For every player a record of this added information is kept:

1. Was the player steady during the game?
2. From what position on the field did the player take shots at the goal?
3. Was the player on the move to help a teammate? Was there teamwork?
4. Did the player tire easily?
5. Did the player know team formations and systems of play?
6. Did the player challenge opponents for a loose ball?
7. Did the player pass well and at the right moment?
8. Did the player trap, block, and tackle well?

SAMPLE SOCCER SCORESHEET
(Boys/Girls Mixed Team)

TEAMS AZTECS VS COMETS

KICKOFF 1 2 3 4

PLAYERS	1ST HALF FG	1ST HALF PG	2ND HALF FG	2ND HALF PG	NO	POSITION	NO	PLAYERS	1ST HALF FG	1ST HALF PG	2ND HALF FG	2ND HALF PG
Judy					32		18	Viki				
Amy	2				40		14	Peggy				
Tony				1	28		11	Joe	2			
Mike					16		29	Tom	2		2	
Criss					10		36	Nancy				
Bobby					17		45	Eleanor				
Beverly					19		12	Dick				
Betty					20		9	Marvin				
Stan					42		15	Patti				
AL					48		21	Janice				
Joan					52		33	Allen				
Mary								Jim				
Dave								Sue				
Greg								Ed				
TIME OUT	~~1~~	~~2~~						TIME OUT	~~1~~	2		

WON BY Comets DATE

SCORE 6-3 PLACE Star Field

RUNNING SCORE	1	2	3	4	5	6
	1	2	3			

9. Did the player show better defensive or offensive work?
10. Was the player injured during the game?

Most teams also have team secretaries or managers. After each game the official scorekeeper gives a report to the managers or secretaries of each team. Copies of the report are then sent to the league commissioner. This commissioner sees that the records are kept as lasting accounts of the games.

Soccer teams have offices where these records are also kept. Coaches study them to investigate the weak and strong points of their players. Then all the players are rated on ability and skill. That's why these records are so important.

PLAYERS STUDY THE RECORDS

The coach posts portions of these records in the players' dressing or meeting room so they may be studied. Players may ask for individual copies so they can study their own records more carefully. Like a teacher, the coach studies these reports to improve the team.

Many times some of this information is also printed in the daily newspapers a day or two before a game.

THE SOCCER PROGRAM

When fans enter a game they usually buy a program. This program looks like a magazine and provides a great deal of information. It gives the names of the players from both teams, their numbers and positions, heights, weights, ages, and a list of substitute players.

The starting line-up is selected from the list of players printed in the official soccer program. The program also lists the team records, and the players' records and their home towns.

PERCENTAGE

The best place to figure percentage is in school. Percentage helps you figure out the team and player standings. Through the percentages shown in the newspapers fans can learn:

1. The teams' standings in the league.
2. The goalkeepers' averages (goals made against goalie).
3. The goalkeepers' saves averages (number of goals saved by goalie).

4. The players' scoring averages.
5. The players' assists averages (player assisting teammate to score).
6. The teams' offensive (scoring) averages.
7. The teams' defensive averages.
8. The teams' penalty (fouls) averages.
9. The teams' offside averages.
10. The players' shots at goal averages.
11. The teams' shots at goal averages.

Team Percentage. To figure the team percentage, or standing, in the league, take *the number of games won and divide by the number of games played.* These problems are carried out to three decimal places.

Example: The Cosmos have played ten games. They have won eight games and lost two. What is the Cosmos' percentage in the league?

$$10\overline{)8.000} = .800$$ —team percentage in the league

GAME RESULTS

Throughout the soccer season the results of the games are printed in the daily newspapers. Reporters print a running account of the games, leading scorers, team standings, leading goalies, and many more statistics and records.

TEAM STANDINGS

Earlier in this chapter you learned about one way a league figures the team percentage. Here is another system that also appears in the sports pages. It is used by the North American Soccer League, which is made up of professional teams.

TEAM STANDINGS

NATIONAL CONFERENCE

Eastern Division

	W	L	GF	GA	BP	Pts.
Cosmos	12	9	46	35	41	113
Lancers	8	11	28	32	27	75
Metros	8	12	25	34	24	72
Diplomats	8	11	21	26	21	69

Central Division

	W	L	GF	GA	BP	Pts.
Tornado	14	7	43	29	40	124
Kicks	12	7	31	21	30	102
Caribous	9	12	34	44	33	87
Roughnecks	10	9	26	26	25	85

Western Division

	W	L	GF	GA	BP	Pts.
Aztecs	14	6	47	31	42	126
Whitecaps	11	8	34	31	31	97
Sounders	9	9	23	21	23	77
Timbers	8	11	28	29	28	76

AMERICAN CONFERENCE

Eastern Division

	W	L	GF	GA	BP	Pts.
Strikers	13	6	31	22	30	108
Fury	12	7	31	21	30	102
Rowdies	10	9	42	34	35	95
Tea Men	10	11	28	36	27	87

Central Division

	W	L	GF	GA	BP	Pts.
Hurricane	14	7	43	29	40	124
Express	13	6	31	22	30	113
Rogues	8	11	21	26	21	69
Sting	7	13	24	34	21	63

Western Division

	W	L	GF	GA	BP	Pts.
Surf	12	7	31	21	30	102
Stompers	10	9	42	34	35	95
Earthquakes	10	11	28	36	27	87
Sockers	10	9	26	26	25	85

Key to Figures: Letter "W" stands for games *won.* Letter "L" means games *lost.* The "GF" means *goals for* the team, and "GA" is for *goals against* the team. The "BP" is for *bonus points,* and "Pts." means *total team points.* Six points are awarded for each win and one bonus point for each goal scored up to a limit of three goals per team per game.

Example: Tornado received 124 total points. This was figured by multiplying 14 times 6 = 84, then adding the 40 bonus points to the 84.

MORE NEWSPAPER AND MAGAZINE RECORDS

Other records often published are:

1. Top ten scorers
2. Top five goalies
3. Players' season figures

TOP TEN SCORERS

PLAYER	TEAM	GAMES	GOALS	ASSISTS	PTS.
Kyle	Cosmos	18	10	10	30
Warren	Aztecs	17	12	5	29
Andy	Lancers	19	11	6	28
Gene	Sting	19	10	5	25
Mike	Strikers	18	12	1	25
Randy	Rowdies	14	9	5	23
Joe	Tornado	14	11	0	22
Richard	Whitecaps	12	8	6	22
Miguel	Timbers	17	9	4	22
Tom	Bicentennials	19	7	4	18

Key: Two points are awarded for each goal, and one point for each assist.

Example: Kyle of the Cosmos scored ten goals, which multiplied times two equals 20. That 20 plus ten assists equals 30 total points for Kyle.

TOP FIVE GOALIES

PLAYER	TEAM	MIN.	SAVES	GOALS	SHUT-OUTS	AVE.
Don	Sounders	1157	78	8	6	0.62
Len	Rowdies	1530	91	17	6	1.00
Art	Aztecs	1695	151	21	7	1.11
Bobby	Strikers	1620	156	21	5	1.17
Ron	Lancers	1620	136	22	5	1.22

Key: To get the goalie percentage, you divide 90 minutes (length of a big-league game) into the total number of goals scored against the goalie. This gives you the goalie's percentage.

Example: Len of the Rowdies played 1530 minutes. Dividing 90 into 1530 = 17. Dividing 17 into 17 goals scored against Len, this gives him a 1.00 (one) goal per game average scored against him.

TEAM PLAYERS SEASON STATISTICS

PLAYER	MINUTES	SHOTS	GOALS	ASSISTS	POINTS
Harvey	1495	12	1	—	2
Don	1710	7	—	—	—
Chuck	1710	26	2	1	5
Tony	1710	10	—	1	1
Len	686	9	—	—	—
Burl	137	5	—	—	—
Jerry	677	21	1	—	2
Ronny	1455	65	7	3	17
Johnny	1635	65	11	6	28
Danny	1620	36	1	9	11
Frank	1112	24	1	3	5
Morris	112	—	—	—	—
Phil	140	7	1	—	2
Paul	1226	27	4	5	13
Derek	1710	3	—	—	—
TEAM TOTALS		317	29	28	86

GOALIES	MINUTES	GAMES	SAVES	GA	AVERAGE
Larry	1157	13	78	8	0.62
Wally	553	7	28	6	1.00

These records show how each player performed in all the games during the soccer season.

How did your team do? How did your team perform? Your opponents? Check with your friends and examine your own records. Ask your parents or teacher to help you figure percentages and averages if you need help. Then work on the game skills in which you show weaknesses.

School, playground, and neighborhood teams keep records, too. You can keep the records of your team and players in your *Soccer Notebook.*

But for the big-league teams, men and women sit at desks all through the soccer season and work on figures and percentages. This work results in the scores and records that make up soccer history.

Write down the soccer history of your school, club, or pick-up team.

14
For the Interested Person Who Can't Play!

The weak, the strong, the young, or old! It makes no difference. *Soccer can be enjoyed by everyone.* Many stories are written about great athletes who were sick or suffered serious accidents or illnesses when they were young.

How did many of these people become successful in later life? Much of their success was possible because they kept physically active in the best way they knew how. Some read sports books; others talked to great soccer players and coaches and worked hard to strengthen their bodies. Later on, as high school and college athletes, they won "All-American" soccer honors. Many well-known people could not play soccer for one reason or another. But this did not stop them from taking part in other ways and enjoying the game.

IF YOU CAN'T PLAY SOCCER

Before young boys and girls go out for soccer, they should get permission from their parents. They should also be *examined by a doctor.* Sometimes a doctor will not allow a person to take part in active sports. So, if you can't play soccer, don't feel sorry for yourself. There are many ways in which you can still take part and enjoy the game.

Follow the Game. Follow the soccer action on TV and radio. Read about soccer in books, magazines, and newspapers.

Help Arrange for Games. Find the right teams for your club to compete against. Be a team secretary. Keep the team records.

Assist the Scorekeeper. Help the scorekeeper with the scorebook and records of your team. Write a report of what every player does on the field. Figure out playing records and percentages.

Be a Reporter. Help with the publicity for your team. Make posters and signs to advertise when and where your team will compete. Report the games to the school and neighborhood newspapers.

Help Take Care of Equipment. Help arrange for the supplies and equipment your team needs. Help mark the soccer field. Help place the corner flags and other equipment before a game and remove them after a game.

Be a Coach's Assistant. Record the names of the starting line-up before game time. Help print the forms for new plays and training rules. This is usually done on an office printing machine.

Practicing Yourself. Are there some skills you wish to practice yourself? With friends? Or with your family? After you decide what you would like to do, talk it over

IF YOU CAN'T PLAY

with your parents. They may wish to ask the doctor if you may do what you have chosen. Have your list of drills ready to show the doctor, so a decision can be made on which ones are allowed.

There are quite a lot of ways you can be active! Whether you are blind, deaf, in a wheelchair, or have other ailments, find out about the kind of programs that are right for you. There are organizations for the physically handicapped, as well as the Joseph P. Kennedy, Jr., foundation for the mentally slow, that sponsor sports and fitness activities for youngsters. These organizations are out to help you! Try them!

IF YOU CAN'T PLAY

Warning. Only after you have the permission of your parents, teacher, or doctor should you make plans to help your team. If your parents and the doctor decide that some of the duties and drills are not for you, remember that a great many other boys and girls do not play soccer, either. You can watch soccer matches on TV or in person, however. It's fun to talk about your favorite goalie, dribbler, striker, or defender. You are still a loyal fan even if you cannot be active physically on the team.

15 Everyone's Off and Kicking

Every year soccer gains popularity in the United States as more and more people learn about the game.

And year after year, you, your friends, and your family can play a part by being active participants.

In playgrounds, backyards, gymnasiums, and fields all over the country, young and old happily play pick-up soccer. They kick short and long passes; they dribble, pivot, and make shots at the goal.

The sports pages of newspapers are filled with stories about new players and old-time favorites. Who will win the school, club, or league title this year?

Boys and girls, men and women, stream onto soccer fields and into the stadiums. They are ready to watch the skillful goalie. They are eager to see the stop-and-go running, heading, dribbling, and shooting of a striker. They buy programs.

Look! Team officials are checking over the field. The teams' starting line-ups run out. They are ready for play!

Listen! There goes the official's whistle. It's time for the kickoff! Come on team! Go! The players are on the move.

Yes. It's soccer time again. Soccer, the great world game.

EVERYONES' KICKING

Glossary

Active Resistance. To apply aggressive pressure in an attempt to win the ball back.

Advantage Rule. A player with the ball is fouled but still has control; the referee allows play to continue.

Angle of Possibility (shooting). The angle formed by drawing imaginary lines from each goal post to the location of the ball. Ball must travel in this area to score a goal.

Assist. A pass to a teammate that results in a goal.

Attacking Team. The team that has possession of the ball.

Back Up. On defense, covering the space behind a teammate in case of an error. Also called supporting a teammate.

Ball Control. The ability to do what you want with the ball.

Banana Kick. Meeting the ball with a slicing instep kick, which causes the ball to curve.

Beat. To go beyond an opponent either by dribbling or passing to a teammate. To put the opponent out of the play.

Block. Using the feet or the body to stop the ball.

Carrying. When the goalkeeper takes more than four steps while holding, bouncing, or throwing the ball.

Center. To pass or kick the ball to the center of the field, usually near the goal.

Center Circle. A ten-yard radius circle drawn in the middle of the boys' field.

Center Line. A straight line in the middle of the field connecting the two sidelines.

Creating Space. Moving in a direction that will open an area for yourself or for a teammate.

Cross. To move the ball from one side of the field to the other side.

Dangerous Play. A play that is likely to cause injury.

Defender. Player (fullback) whose main duty is to protect the goal area.

Defensive Stance. The well-balanced defensive positioning of a player's body and feet which makes the player ready to tackle the ball at the right moment.

Delay. To slow down the offensive team so your teammates have time to get back in the defensive positions.

Direct Free Kick. A place kick that can result in a score when kicked directly at the goal.

Double Pass. When the passer receives a return pass from a teammate.

Double Foul. A rule is broken at the same time by a member of each team, for which a drop ball is awarded.

Draw an Opponent. The art of forcing an opponent toward you and out of position or responsibility to play.

Dribbling. To move the ball along the ground with the feet without losing control.

Drop Ball. An official puts the ball back into play by dropping it to the ground between any two players except the goalie.

End Line. The end-of-field boundary lines marking the short side of the field where the goal posts are located.

Fake. Forcing an opponent to move toward you but in the wrong direction.

Far Post. The goal post that is farthest away from you when you approach the goal for an angle shot.

Feeder. A player whose main duty is to get the ball to a high scoring player on his team.

Feint. The same as a fake.

F.I.F.A. Federation of International Football Association. Organization that regulates world soccer rules.

First Time. To kick or pass the ball to a teammate without first trapping it.

Flat Front. Players attacking or defending against opponents in a straight line across the field.

Forward. An offensive player; also known as an attacker or a striker.

Goalie. The goalkeeper; also known as keeper.

Goalkeeper. The goalie or keeper. The last defender of the goal who may use hands to catch or block the ball in the penalty area.

Goal Kick. An indirect free kick taken by the defensive team from a spot nearest to where the ball crossed the goal line.

Goal Line. The same as the end line, but more specifically between the goal posts.

Goal Posts. Two upright posts eight feet high on which the crossbar is attached.

Half-volley. To kick the ball instantly after it hits the ground.

Handling. A girl contacting the ball purposely with the hand or any part of the arm when the hands and arms are not in complete contact against the chest area.

Hands. When a player intentionally touches the ball with the arms or hands.

Hat Trick. When one player on a team scores three goals in one game.

Heading. To strike the ball with the head or forehead.

Holding. To prevent the progress of a player by placing a hand or arm on an opposing player.

Immediate Chase. Defensive strategy to win the ball back quickly after the team has lost control of it.

Indirect Free Kick. A free kick awarded by the official in which a goal *may not* be scored directly from the kick. The ball must first touch another player before entering the goal.

Inside Striker. An offensive player, also known as an attacker, who is nearest the opponent's goal and has the main responsibility of scoring goals.

Jockey. A way to cover an opponent with the ball by feinting without committing.

"Keeper." Slang for goalkeeper.

Kick. To make the ball travel with the foot.

Kick-off. Starting the game from the center of the field. Used to start each period of play and after each score.

Lead. To pass the ball into a space in front of the receiver.

Link Player. A halfback or midfielder whose main duties are to "link" the offensive players with the defensive players.

Lob. To loft the ball into the air.

Mark. To guard an opponent closely.

Midfielders. Players also known as "link" players whose duties are to play between the strikers and attackers.

Near Post. The nearest goal post to you when approaching the goal at an angle.

Obstruct. To hinder the movement of an opponent by getting in the way of the run. This can be made legal or illegal.

Offside. When a player is ahead of the ball and doesn't have two players between himself or herself and the opponent's goal.

One-Touch. A method by which a player controls the ball and passes to a teammate all in one motion.

Outside Striker. An offensive player, also known as an attacker, assigned to play near the sidelines.

Over-dribbling. Controlling the ball by dribbling too often and too long during the game.

Pass. To kick or head the ball to another teammate.

Penalty Kick. A direct free kick taken from a spot directly in front of the goal.

Penetration. Either the ball or a player advances quickly through the defense, usually to set up a scoring opportunity.

Play-it-back. Passing the ball to an unmarked teammate behind you.

Playmaker. A player whose major responsibility is feeding passes, especially on offense.

Restraining Lines. A straight line connecting the sidelines; on each side of the center line of a girls' soccer field.

Running Off the Ball. Intelligent movement to position yourself and help a teammate who has the ball.

Save. To prevent a score by blocking or deflecting the ball out of the goal.

Scoring Chance. An opportunity to score a goal.

Screen. Legally getting in the way (obstructing) of the opponent and the ball.

Set-up. To kick or pass the ball in such a way as to give a teammate a better chance of scoring.

Shooting. Forcing a kicked ball toward the goal.

Sideline. The boundary line marking the long side of the playing area, connecting the goal lines at either end of the field.

Six-yarder. A goal kick.

Space. An open area where the offense can develop.

Stance. The position of a player's feet, arms, hands, and body.

Striker. An offensive player, also known as an attacker, who usually set up plays and takes shots for a goal.

Strong Foot. A player's best kicking foot.

Style of Play. Long or short passing and hustling.

Support. Helping a teammate who has the ball from the rear.

Switch. Two players changing positions on the field.

Tackle. An attempt to take the ball away from an opponent or cause an opponent to rush a pass.

Target Player. A player placed near the goal to whom teammates try to direct the ball.

Through-pass. A pass between defenders, usually into the space behind one of them.

Throw-in. An opponent puts the ball back into play after it goes over the sideline.

Touch Line. Same as the sideline.

Trailer. A player on the team who is in a support position.

Trap. To control the ball with the feet.

Two Touch. A method of soccer that allows a player to control the ball on the first touch and pass or shoot on the second touch.

USSF. United States Soccer Federation; the governing body of soccer in the United States.

Wall. A defensive move to assist the goalie on a free kick near the goal area. The defenders line up ten yards from the ball, shoulder to shoulder and attempt to block a kick.

Wall Pass. A "give-and-go" play where the ball is passed to a teammate who immediately returns it.

Weak Foot. The foot with which the player has the least amount of skill to kick, dribble, or tackle.

Wing. Players assigned to play near the sidelines.

Zone Defense. When defenders cover certain areas of the field rather than a particular player.

Index